# WHAT AWESOME HUMANS ARE SAYING ABOUT THIS BOOK...

*"Here we have another 'must-have' book for anyone with a desire to create a great work experience. In her usual direct but succinct manner, Simone communicates the key ingredients to help employers and employees thrive. This book comes at just the right time."*

**MARK CATCHLOVE**
Director, Global Insight Group, Herman Miller

*"It might seem commonplace to argue that workplaces need to be human-centric – Google it and you'll be rewarded with more than nine million search results. So, why another book about the human-centric workplace? Because Simone Fenton-Jarvis' perspective is passionate and personal, enriched with stories and drawing on her own experiences, written in a unique and authentic way, as if she was explaining this to you personally over a cuppa. She is diving deep, citing widely from Marx to Socrates, from Freud to Krugman, but always stays down to earth and makes issues relatable. If you want to truly understand what it means to bring your full self to work, how the brain is both rational and emotional, what good leadership looks like, how to detect a supportive workplace culture and what roles space and technology play, this book is for you."*

**DR KERSTIN SAILER**
Professor in the Sociology of Architecture,
The Bartlett School of Architecture, University College London

"The future of work everywhere is deeply and resolutely interwoven with our thriving as human beings. Simone Fenton-Jarvis addresses the very real (and all too common) barriers to putting people first in order to get results. Practical and wise, The Human-Centric Workplace *is a must-read for leaders about what really matters at work right now.*"

**MOE CARRICK**
*Author of* Fit Matters *(2017) and* Bravespace Workplace *(2019)*

"A very personal story that cuts to the chase of why human beings being human should be core to organizations."

**LINDA HAUSMANIS**
*CEO, Institute of Workplace and Facilities Management*

"After such an extraordinary 18 months where the world of workplace changed overnight, Simone has delivered a timely, inspirational, thought-provoking read. She uses a wealth of personal experience and the latest psychology insights to rethink the purpose of the workplace and how we can create spaces that allow us to bring our best to every visit."

**ANTONY WILTSHIRE**
*Director of Workplace, UK&I, Edelman*

"The power of people is our biggest strength in business and in society. The Human-Centric Workplace *takes this principle and explores how we should, and can, make it an intrinsic part of culture and leadership and how, by harnessing this power and connection, people and society will flourish.*"

**JOANNA SWASH**
*Group CEO, Moneypenny*

"As a student of the classics, sociology and neuroscience, I find that people sometimes struggle with translating theory into practice. This book bridges that gap: Simone gives us research, data, storytelling, personal examples, key takeaways and questions for us to reflect upon.

"If you're one of those people for whom it's no longer enough just to say, 'Yep, that happens to me, too,' then here you'll find ideas to help you change your space (wherever that may be) so that your workplace suits who you are as a human being, not a human doing.

"Jim Rohn said, 'The book you don't read won't help you.' I urge you to read this one armed with pen and paper; scribble notes, fold down corners, ask yourself the questions and, when you have the answers, do something about them."

**LIZ KENTISH**
*Managing Director, Kentish & Co*


"A powerful and brilliantly thought-provoking call to arms on the power of applying human principles and fostering people's best thinking. I thought I understood this topic before, but this book had me writing pages of notes to self!"

**CHRIS WALTON**
*Managing Director, UK, Ireland and Nordics, CEVA Logistics*

"Simone digs deep into human behaviour and what that brings to the workplace, explaining her thoughts in her own insightful and straightforward way, with plenty of academic references. The book is well structured with handy reference tables, practical advice, key takeaways and reflections that act as useful reminders. A must-read book to realign and centre our thinking on the human aspect of work and place, and to move away from the binary debate of work location."

**DAVID GEORGE**
*Managing Director, iPWC Ltd*

"Simone Fenton-Jarvis provides us all with a timely and urgent reminder that culture isn't just the latest business trend but, in fact, the reverse.

"Business is just the latest cultural trend. Humans and culture were here first. Organizations would do well to recalibrate their structure and priorities with the profound and compelling case presented in The Human-Centric Workplace *if they wish to optimize performance, employee experience and customer expectations."*

**MICHAEL HENDERSON**
*Corporate Anthropologist, Cultures AT Work,*
*author of Above the Line (2014)*

*"Simone brings a freshness to a complex and (recently) much talked about topic by focusing on its most important element – people. Because of this, she is able to address a range of social and environmental issues linked to the ways we work and live. Crucially, she is drawing on her own experience as a pioneer of new working cultures to point a way ahead for us all."*

**MARK ELTRINGHAM**
Publisher of Workplace Insight and IN Magazine

*"Many people talk about the workplace. Simone Fenton-Jarvis lives and breathes the workplace. This book is a great read. It provides insight and guidance for everyone and I have no doubt it will help shape workplaces of the future."*

**JULIE KORTENS**
Chair of Judges IWFM Impact Awards

*"At times astonishing, at other times perfectly observed; Simone Fenton-Jarvis has created an outstanding and timely call to arms."*

**BRUCE DAILEY**
Author of The Joy of Work (2019) and
Podcast Host, Eat Sleep Work Repeat

Published by
**LID Publishing**
An imprint of LID Business Media Ltd.
The Record Hall, Studio 304,
16-16a Baldwins Gardens,
London EC1N 7RJ, UK

info@lidpublishing.com
www.lidpublishing.com

A member of:

BPR
businesspublishersroundtable.com

Printed by Severn, Gloucester
ISBN: 978-1-911671-62-6
ISBN: 978-1-911671-63-3 (ebook)

Cover and page design: Caroline Li

ENABLING PEOPLE,
COMMUNITIES AND OUR
PLANET TO THRIVE

# THE
# HUMAN-
# CENTRIC
# WORKPLACE

SIMONE FENTON-JARVIS

MADRID | MEXICO CITY | LONDON
NEW YORK | BUENOS AIRES
BOGOTA | SHANGHAI | NEW DELHI

# ACKNOWLEDGEMENTS

I have met and worked with so many inspirational people, many of whom who will (hopefully) read this book and look back at all the discussions and shared experiences; there are lots of thanks to give to my awesome tribe!

Kate, there are not many words to describe what you mean to me and how grateful I am for your unwavering support and belief in me. I am sorry for all the evenings and weekends that I left you watching Christmas films and reruns of *Friends*, and still, not once did you tell me to stop writing. Patsy, for sitting with me (mainly sleeping) throughout the long days and nights, and for the long walks to clear my head.

My two stars, Sarah and Gail, for always being there, always encouraging and always being proud, especially when I could literally not see you throughout the months that I was writing this book – 'bloody pandemic'.

To the dream team: PT, you will never accept the part you played over the last few years, but I am going to tell you anyway. You showed me that Human Leadership was not just a figment of my imagination, but that it is possible to achieve, with conscious effort, time, vulnerability, belief, trust, and safety. Thank you for being my agent, my agony aunt, my sounding board, my safe place. TJ and WH, from colleagues, to friends. Dream teams are not easy to form – you have been awesome, there is more on you guys later in the book!

Norma, for giving me my first job in FM and being a mentor and friend ever since. Thank you for accepting, encouraging and fine tuning my lack of sugar coating during difficult situations and for reminding me that it is good to admit you don't know things. I am not sure if we will ever get there, but at least we can say that we gave it our all.

Mel Bull for accepting me onto the MBA course all those years ago and enriching my life ever since with your positive ball of energy and awesome humanness.

To a bunch of absolute kick ass women who have inspired me, paved the way, mentored, listened and been all round superhuman beings: Julie Kortens, Moe Carrick, Liz Kentish, Nikki Lathbury and Lucy Hind.

In 2019, I sat down with Amanda Cookson and hashed out my ten year plan with my main goal being to write a book. I never expected to accomplish it within two years – thank you for all the support, inspiration, and awesomeness.

Neil Usher, Natasha Wallace, Nigel Oseland, Perry Timms and Andy Swann, I hope my writing inspires people as much as yours has me.

A thanks to Mark Catchlove, one of the nicest blokes I have ever encountered, for reminding people that we are more than our job titles and for his ongoing support and encouragement.

Mark Eltringham, Matt Tucker, Antony Slumbers, Martin Read, Will Easton, Sandra Panara, Ali Kahn, Chris Moriarty, Ian Ellison and James Pinder for the thought leadership and the challenging of thinking.

To my long standing friend Leon Snell, work wife Amy Wood, the PA I never realised I needed until it was too late – Ella Constantine, Helen Fulson, Emily Green, Jon Wynn, Kate Swarbs, Tim Elgar, crazy uncle Jon and Team Twinkl, you all played varying and important parts along the way, thank you so much. A big thank you to the team at LID for your support, encouragement, knowledge and passion.

And finally, thank you to all who those that dehumanize workplaces: you spurred me on to forge a better world.

# WHAT'S INSIDE?

# FOREWORD
# BY DR MEL BULL

"I am a small, noisy, smiley blonde girl." You may look through that list of words and recognize yourself in some or all of them, but this is how I have heard myself being referred to. Yes, I absolutely acknowledge these attributes are representative of me; however, it is how they are inferred that may change. Sometimes they can be said in a positive way, and other times in a negative way! How we choose to refer to or engage with other human beings has always intrigued me, whether this be through understanding our Jungian[1] preferences or whether this be through our interpersonal communication; but why do we feel the need to judge or to stereotype? Argyris[2] discussed the ladder of inference, which evidences how quickly we can rush to judgment and actions based on limited data. We seem to be losing the art of listening, instead making candid judgments on what someone is wearing and how they look rather than actively listening to what they are saying. Is a world where we all hear each other without judgment a eutopia? Or is this about realigning how we 'are' in the world? Simone has tried to explore these concepts from an authentic place of being a young woman with a successful career who has tried to remain true to herself at every turn.

Being human in the workplace allows us to be who we are, to understand how culture can influence the environment in the organization, more than the physical space itself. When we talk about the workplace, are we focusing on the physical? Do we also need to focus on the impact of the intangible environment to provide a new lens? This intangible environment is all about the culture, and this is created by the leadership of the organization and the behaviours that become instilled in the social actors within it. We need to challenge the norm, be curious and start to really listen and learn from each other, challenging inappropriate or 'bad' behaviour wherever this appears in the organization. What part of yourself do you leave at home when you go to work? Are you forcing yourself into a position of emotional labour by not bringing *yourself* to work on a daily basis.[3] How safe is it to bring your whole self to work in your current environment?

The discussion in the book also focuses on some insights into how our brain works and potentially how this affects how we lead. We have all had leaders who have either inspired or killed our motivation – why did this happen? There are opportunities to reflect on these moments as you work your way through the book – to truly understand the why. If you are a leader, and this for me does not necessarily mean a leader by 'rank,' how do you engage, create curiosity and challenge the status quo? How do you motivate the individuals who form your team in the workplace?

In my view, it has never been so important to be human. We have faced an international pandemic that has impacted every person in the world, we have a common factor that is relative to all. So, what does that mean as we move forward? The meaning of hybrid working is being discussed around the world, and now more than ever, we need to be kind to each other, recognize when this can be applied and when it cannot, and ensure you have a good reason why somebody is required to be sat in an office every day. Simone discusses how these different ways of working have been interpreted and also applied by different organizations, and for me the main area here is that we trust our workers when we cannot see them. This is a challenge for managers globally. But why wouldn't you trust your team members to work from home, why do you need to physically see them sitting at a desk? We have all proved over the last year that we can engage in remote working and still produce work to the highest level, but how do we maintain the links with each other? As human beings, we crave a level of social interaction, and this may be on different levels; as a screaming extrovert, I most definitely do not want to be in my study five days a week, 52 weeks a year; but my partner is perfectly happy working this way and connecting with his work colleagues via Microsoft Teams! However, this comes back down to who we are, the jobs we do and the culture of our organization.

To enhance the employee experience, we need to ensure we are working together from the leadership of the organization through to HR and Facilities Management and beyond. Let us stop working in silos and have a joined-up approach to put people at the heart of everything we do. If we can show this through the leadership of the organization, we can start to embed the evolution of the employee as a whole person who is central to everything we do and not just a cog in the wheel.

To address these areas I have raised in the foreword of this book, there is some clear guidance through Simone's Human-Centric Workplace Playbook and I for one have found them to be an interesting and useful tool. Let us not give up now; we have come too far to just return to the old norm. Let us create the new normal together, ensuring there is mutual respect, a safe environment (physically and mentally) and give ourselves a real chance to bring our whole selves to work to create the new future.

**DR MEL BULL**
Assistant Head of Postgraduate and
Executive Education, Nottingham Trent Business School

# WELL,
# HELLO THERE!

Let me start by introducing my 'why,' not just for writing this book but in life. Council Estates in the North of England get a bad rap, as do underachieving schools and single-parent homes, but for me they were just stereotypes. My roots were strong, and I had many people around me to nourish me and keep me standing up tall and straight during the storms. I am all too aware of how easily life could have headed down a different path from where I am today without the good people around me.

I was raised to be a nice person with values and principles, to have manners and integrity, to embrace a challenge, to be grateful, to laugh and to always say what I think. I was always told by my nanna, "The sky is the limit" and as such I grew up with the belief that everything could always be better and nothing or nobody could get in the way of what I knew was right or what I wanted; it just needed a bit of good old northern grit.

From age seven I began playing football; this was the '90s and women's football was a different experience to what it is now, with too many stereotypes and not enough opportunities, funding, role models or equality.

During a PE lesson when I requested that I play football instead of netball, my teacher encouraged me to do so and focus not only on what I was good at, but what I enjoyed. During one lesson a boy mocked me, and my teacher replied, "Simone can do whatever she likes, you just focus on being the goalie." I was seven years old, and to this day I can remember where I was standing, where my teacher was standing, what the playground looked like and the look on the boy's face when my teacher stood up for me. To this day, she has no idea how important that moment was to me.

When I started secondary school, again I was the odd one out, the girl who played football. Simon, the tomboy, the lesbian, and a few other unimaginative names. My PE teacher was a football fan; I would rush to find her on a Monday morning to talk about the weekend's football. I recall many conversations and banter of how bad Oldham Athletic was (I keep the faith) and how Manchester United had only won thanks to 'Fergie time.'

My PE teacher actively encouraged me to join in with the boys' PE lessons. She set up a girl's school team and brought many smiles to my face when she saw me and called me "super Simeone." The moments of normality, the relationship and connection, the interest, the support – it all powered my Teflon coating, keeping me going at times when school life was far from easy. These experiences played out again many years later within the workplace – more on this later.

Having the two role models, both female, who both taught PE, inspired me to want to do the same, but, well, as you have probably worked out by now, it was not the career for me. To have a job where I remained active and utilized my skills and experiences, I started to work within Leisure Management. Yes, like so many, I ended up working in Facilities Management by accident.

I continued to spur on playing football, too, and throughout more than 20 years, I fought tooth and nail to simply just play a sport that I loved. A decision that came with bullying, discrimination, stereotyping, many lost weekends and frustrations, but lots of amazing experiences and life lessons.

Well, there are no rainbows without rain, and I remember a lot of weekends spent in the rain.

I played at a high level alongside some amazing people and had the pleasure to be captain, be player manager and a club director at several clubs. I learned the true feeling of what it was like to win and lose as a team, the impact and importance of leadership and dependability, a sense of belonging, individual skills, respect, resilience, loyalty, communication, learning from and embracing mistakes, having fun and what it meant to be brave. I also learned discipline and the importance of preparation.

My career in FM was going well. I pushed myself to learn, to understand, to be curious, always asking why, and to always wanting better. My career was progressing quickly, and I threw myself into many deep ends (not literally, despite managing swimming pools), continued to challenge myself and those around me, and stood up for what was right, which was never easy at the time. I will talk about more of this later in the book.

Right up to today, where I work as the Workplace Consultancy Director for a global organization, my upbringing, what I experienced and learned through sport and the early days of my career, underpins not just my leadership style, but my whole being. I remain true to my values and have never demanded that people should follow me. In fact, in my own true way I have raced ahead, but when I have turned around I have been so happy, grateful and relieved to see I was not alone. My tribe has always been strong, and knowing that, right down to my core, has enabled me to continue to push forward.

Following mixed experiences of the world of work through being managed, being a leader and through mentoring, I have often questioned why I become so frustrated with some of the things I hear, see and feel. The frustration sometimes bubbles over, not in an angry throwing chairs kind of way, more of an inner rage that drives me into a bubble, working longer hours, to fix the world. Working with a coach helped me to embrace the frustration as a positive; in fact, I even have a little reminder stuck to my laptop:

I have also learned that, as much as I am a human who gets frustrated when there is a values and/or behaviours clash, the person who is frustrating me is also a human, entitled to their own values, behaviours and ways of being, is potentially somebody who does not know any differently and is simply just doing their best. Mutual respect of differences makes the world go round, and my nanna always reminded me of letting go of things that you cannot change with the saying:

God, grant me the serenity to accept the things I cannot change,
Courage to change the things I can,
and Wisdom to know the difference.
(Reinhold Niebuhr, 1932)

What does it mean to be human? What does it mean to be a human at work? The answers to these questions should not be dissimilar: to have a purpose, to connect, belong and to feel, and yet, organizational cultures still do not embrace people bringing their whole selves to work. If we are not showing up, not bringing our whole awesome selves, we are not thriving; we are, in fact, hiding.

This all starts with leadership. A person being good at a job does not mean they will be a good leader, and yet, organizations continue to promote people not just past their task performance capability but past their human skills capabilities. Leaders of the 21st century need empathy and listening skills, to be brave and embrace vulnerability. Good leaders use these skills to instil a sense of team community, camaraderie, empowerment and trust. People will only thrive when their heart, mind and gut are aligned and on the same journey; good leaders provide a vision of the destination, not a map and a compass.

Following the year of the largest remote working experiment, not many would argue against work not being somewhere we go but what we do and the why we do it; the way we work will never be the same again. Employees across sectors, verticals and continents are demanding change. Purpose, values and organizational cultures are being challenged. Organizations treating people as a means for financial performance must change; the organization can and should be the vehicle to drive the development of people, societies and the planet. We must take responsibility and act starting now.

Organizations must adapt to the new reality in which leaders from HR, IT and Facilities Management and Workplace need to collaborate closely to create a culture that is more caring, more productive and, above all, human, and is reflected within the spaces, technology and the processes.

The workplace and leadership are the root cause and fuel of so many societal issues including wellbeing, inequality, the economy and the climate. *The Human-Centric Workplace* highlights that organizations through to lone individuals have the power to be the change and drive the change. Culminating with a playbook, *The Human-Centric Workplace* seeks to inform and inspire action through demystifying the 'what,' the 'why' and the 'how' to ensure our people, businesses, communities and planet thrive.

Some will read this book and think it is a romanticized view of the workplace – I am an optimistic person who knows we can do better, and we must do better. We do not have to do everything; we just must be human and act now. There is nothing wrong with aiming for the moon and landing among the stars; there is something wrong if we aim for toxic waste ground and be happy when we land right in it. In order for companies to thrive and not just survive, the workplace of the future will be one of psychological safety, listening, learning opportunities, connectedness to others, personal development, respect and caring for the planet. It is by allowing employees to bring their whole selves to work that will result in positive wellbeing throughout the workforce and a greater engagement in their work and the company.

There are so many excellent human-centric workplaces out there, and so many awful ones and I have worked with workplaces right across the spectrum. It is worth me noting that I have intentionally avoided 'naming names' throughout this book; these are my experiences and my stories from 15 years in the industry working across global organizations right down to organizations of a few hundred people.

This book is a call to action, a plea, to anybody who leads or has a desire to lead in the future. I hope it will inspire you to inspire others and drive change for the betterment of everybody, the wider society and the planet. We all have a part to play.

# CHAPTER 1

# TO BE A
# HUMAN

"Wanting to understand who we are, where we come from and how we evolved is part of what makes us human."[4]

What does it mean to be a human? A not-so-simple question that unwraps complexity that humanity continues to grapple with. What separates us from other species? What is our purpose? From poets, philosophers, anthropologists, religious bodies, scientists, politicians and artists to every person out there following a little gin (surely not just me?). Despite the efforts, the answers are diverse and nonconclusive, because believing in a single answer would create silos between the brain, emotion, the body and so forth; we must consider the many angles that make up the whole human.

Karl Marx believed that humans are social creatures and therefore can only develop within a society. Like Marx, Plato also believed that human nature is social, that we derive satisfaction from our social relationships, that we need others. Plato believed in souls, the immaterial mind and the material body composed of reason (the physical) and will (the emotional). For Plato, the soul was the source for everything we feel – love, anguish, anger, ambition, fear. And most of our mental conflict as humans are caused by these aspects not being in harmony. For Aristotle, writing in the 4th century BCE, to be human meant having a goal, to belong and to live a happy life.[5]

David Hume believes in perceptions of truth and moments of realization that alter consciousness. Ludwig Wittgenstein[6] writes that it is our ability to think consciously, and to be human is to think – true, false – it does not truly matter. In the early 17th century, René Descartes, whose famous statement, "I think, therefore I am" implied only humans possess minds, whereas animals act on instincts.

Peterson[7] explains how anthropologist Clifford Geertz refers to human nature as 'unfinished' because we require culture to complete us, to make us fully human. To be human is shaped by the interactions between individuals and their settings, between the natural and the social worlds. "There can be no universal human, no human species-being in any true sense." Geertz concludes that culture, the symbols and structures, determine what it means to be human and thus without culture, there is no humanity.

"What makes the human superior to field animals?" ruminated King Solomon (10th century BCE). Humans are not the only species that walk on two legs, we do not have the largest brain and we are not the only ones who have Facilities Management functions – just check out how badgers create environments to live and to thrive.

Chimps kiss, laugh, lie, have in-group politics and have goals. Ants, wolves and dolphins show social traits and elephants cry and grieve. African buffalos even form a circle around a female giving birth to protect her from predators. We have become increasingly aware that all these human traits started evolving millions of years before the first human descended and that any human traits are advanced animal instincts.

There are many things that make humans special in relation to the rest of the millions of species within the animal kingdom: speech, our remarkable brains, opposable thumbs, we are the only species that blush, we remain in the care of our parents much longer than other living primates (my dad in particular!) and we have lives after our reproduction years have finished.

We are the only species to think about the long-term future.[8] We are a remarkable species when considering that, according to estimations, 99.9% of all the species that have ever lived are now extinct.[9] As David Attenborough said regrettably, "This is now our planet, run by human-kind for humankind. There is little left for the rest of the living world."[10] Humans have not only survived, but they also rule and have seen and driven the intellectual and technological progress beyond any other form of existence.

> "To be human is to experience life in all its colours and potential, the awe of being alive and the thrill of discovering what it means to be us, the greatest wonder in the world."[11]

Ultimately, asking what it means to be human does not result in answers, only more questions. A question that once came from philosophy is now tangled in politics, justice, identity and every molecule of our existence. From connection, empathy, creativity and consciousness to laughter and love, the pure miracle of life and feeling alive, it cannot be fully explained, but it can be felt.

## BRING YOUR HUMAN

> "My humanity is bound up in yours, for we can only be human together."[12]

In the early days of our 300,000-year human evolution, work was simple: we worked to eat and avoid being eaten. Meaning and purpose came from elsewhere, whether it was spirituality, art, religion or science. As humankind has evolved, our identities, such as parent, friend, nationality, religious beliefs, hobbies and our careers have become intertwined. Work is no longer about survival; work has become an extension of our identity.

Social connectedness, culture, belonging, purpose, the ability to think – these are not things that simply stop when somebody is working. Neither does our lifestyle, our responsibilities, worries, fears or anxieties. Yet somehow, we have been hooked into believing that when at work we must diminish such humanity and appear robotic.

The most underused asset at work in the 21$^{st}$ century? Being human.

The ways and the amount of human that you and others bring to work is yours and their choice. When we show up physically, psychologically, emotionally and spiritually, we bring our minds and the wonderful qualities that make us all unique.

Humans have advanced consciousness, the quality that makes us aware, to perceive and ponder. Morality tells us what is right and wrong and curiosity sparks our brains. We adorn many positive behaviours, such as empathy to see things from somebody else's perspective, love, passion, creativity, feelings, common sense, optimism, fear, joy, storytelling, kindness, humility and respect.

There are downsides of human behaviour, too: the lies, aggression and violence, theft, cheating, bullying and harassment, stress, gossiping and rumours, objectification, whining and negativity and selfishness. It is both the positive and the negative that define humanness.

The saying "If you can't handle me at my worst, then you don't deserve me at my best" springs to mind here. Okay, I never expected to quote Marilyn Monroe and I am aware that this is usually shared in a form of a meme following a relationship break-up. But work relationships are real relationships and can be as equally as painful.

With the exponential rise of technology within the workplace, which is showing no signs of slowing, humans have a unique opportunity to offer something different and compelling within the workplace and society as a whole: to be human, to connect on a deeper emotional level.

I recall one experience when I was working long hours and attending my workplace outside of normal operating hours and regularly covering sickness, all unpaid. At the time I did not think much of it. I was always greeted with gratitude, I loved the role, the organization, the customers and my colleagues and I was giving my all; my purpose was clear. I knew the importance of my attendance; it did not need financial rewards. If I were to describe my behaviour and attitude, it was one of commitment, loyalty and passion.

However, some things were not reciprocal; in fact, when I had a dentist appointment, my manager said if I were going to be longer than one hour then I would need to book half a day's holiday. At the time I only had one day of annual leave left to last six more weeks. I told my manager I was planning on taking a long weekend as I was feeling tired and asked if I could just make the time up as I would only be a couple hours. The answer was no.

Three days later, I received a phone call at 4am from my manager. I lived the closest to the workplace and was always the one who was asked to attend out of hours. I silenced my phone, rolled over and said a couple of expletives as I convinced myself to try and go back to sleep. After a few minutes I realized I was wide awake, and the guilt was pumping through my veins. Despite feeling let down, I just could not allow myself to lower myself to my manager's level.

I went to work and was greeted by quite a serious incident, which took a few hours to resolve. By that point I was due on shift. I asked my manager if I could pop home, as I had rushed out of the house – the answer was no. I believe it was that day that I truly realized that if you look after your people, they will look after you. Within a few months, I left the organization.

With any workplace there will be lies, gossip and bad habits, but also creativity, innovation, connection, passion, inspiration and love. A human-centric workplace is not a perfect workplace; they do not exist yet (I am an optimistic soul!) but the difference between a human-centric workplace and a toxic workplace is that, within the human-centric workplace, the bad behaviours are not accepted, they do not blend in, they are not the norm, and they are called out and stopped before permeating others and becoming the norm or the expected.

"... the diversity and imperfection of human souls is, ultimately, what makes institutions engaging, humane and habitable ... human systems are imperfect, the homes for unsolvable problems ..."[13]

The concept of human-centric workplaces is not a new one. Let us look at IBM and their very apt strapline "IBM set the trends – before they became trends." People centricity is not a trend or a fad to IBM, it is part of its DNA:

"Even in the difficult early years of IBM, from 1916 to 1922, when founder Thomas Watson Sr. needed bank loans to cover the payroll, the company found a way to fund employee education. Watson clearly saw the shortest path to success for IBM was through the success of IBM employees."[14]

Equal pay was in place in 1935, paid annual leave from 1937, a formal equal opportunities policy was launched in 1953, adoption assistance from 1972 and flexible working from 1980. Today, IBM spends over US $450 million annually on its training and development program, with each employee averaging 77 hours of formal training. Programs such as 'basic blue' provides new managers with the skills they need to create effective and engaging working environments.[15]

You will either have had, or have heard stories, where soft skills have been labelled as 'fluffy,' where emotions have been a weakness greeted by eye rolls and where there is an expectation that your 'personal life' should be left at the door of the office. Humans do not and should not function like this.

The 'soft' has often been associated with women, and this gender bias has resulted in challenges for both men and women, and everybody in between. Nobody is winning when a man is described as assertive, yet a woman with the same behaviours is described as bossy.

The words we say and hear matter and, during 2019, a campaign started, #biascorrect, which pushed back against some of the labels being used for women in business such as bossy, aggressive, pushy, cold, calculated, emotional, quiet and shrill. This lose-lose dichotomy between too forceful and too timid echoes so much of the research (and my own experiences!). The time to call out such behaviour is well overdue. No matter your gender, do not accept it – we can do better and we must do better, everybody can play there part in being an ally for a better world.

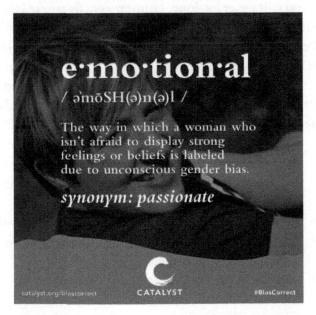

During the 2020/2021 pandemic, the subsequent questioning that followed of "What is it we go to an office for?" led to an increase in talk of the need for better workplaces, human-centric workplaces. As a fellow workplace professional, wise woman, all-round good egg and source of inspiration, Sandra Panara, passionately said recently, "If we are not providing workplaces for humans, what are we doing?" I am with Sandra on this; albeit there are good intentions from many, we are getting it wrong.

As the wonderful Moe Carrick highlighted, "It's not rocket science to understand what it takes to design and lead a workplace fit for human life, but it's not easy, either."[16]

Like the many times I wore a number seven football shirt and practiced free kicks dreaming of being the David Beckham of women's football, organizations cannot just dress the workplace walls with branding that claims they are human centric and stop there. Human-centric workplaces take skill, a team effort, lots of practice and the mindset that you will never be done. Human-centric workplaces are about integrity, values and, quite simply, not being a d*ck.

People are not just cogs in your organization's machine, merely existing to drive your organization's financial success. People do not want to be managed, controlled and worn down. The employee experience has evolved and continues to do so.

→ Everybody deserves to be seen, heard and known.
→ Everybody deserves the opportunity to develop their skills and use their talents.
→ Everybody deserves to be led, inspired and empowered.
→ Everybody has the right to return home from work each day feeling fulfilled.
→ Nobody is merely a means to a company's financial success.

→ Everybody deserves to thrive.
→ Everybody deserves to feel and have those feelings acknowledged.
→ We are all humans.

I recollect one situation when I had spent weeks working on a project, and when I presented it my boss did not just rip it apart, he ripped me apart in the process. It was not what he said but the way he said it; it was the disappointment I felt that somebody I had so much respect for now stood in front me being everything I did not want them to be. The accusatory and undermining tone was experienced by somebody who was passionate about the project and felt they had given their all; I was frustrated and tired, and a few tears rolled down my face. I told them how I felt I was not trusted, and the feedback felt misplaced. I was told that being emotional and dramatic was not the answer and that I cared too much.

I had experienced plenty of situations where male colleagues had been given feedback and told to make some alterations; why was I on the receiving end of such a dressing down and consequent labels? So many years later, I still wonder what they thought was wrong with the work (I never did receive constructive feedback), yet I feel angry knowing that this was very likely to be gender bias mixed with a lack of emotional intelligence and poor leadership skills.

If you take anything from reading this book, let it be that no leader should ever make one of their team members feel like they should care less. NEVER.

The same thinking, experiences and examples apply to discriminations such as disability, race, religion, age, sexual orientation, colour, and lifestyle choices such as tattoos, hair colour, piercings and dietary choices. The very nature of humans is that we are diverse, but sadly, it is also a fact that where there is difference, often driven by fear of the unknown and feeling threatened, we look to divide. While there are examples of such bias and discrimination, people are prevented from bringing their whole self to work.

Being a human at work enables and empowers equality and opportunity, the human-centric workplace ensures that you are comfortable to express yourself when and how you choose; warts and all, with no apologies.

## YOU BE YOU; I WILL BE ME

Genetics, personality, our physical appearance, our attitude and values, perspectives and experiences, habits, intellect, life goals and relationships. We are all one of a kind – the uniqueness comes from within and is demonstrated in our actions and behaviours. Despite the uniqueness, "we are far more united and have far more in common with each other than things that divide us."[17] And yet, we divide ourselves into groups of 'us' and 'them' or the 'in group' and the 'out group.' The us-and-them attitude is one that is prevalent throughout our lives: labour versus conservative, plant-based versus meat eaters, Manchester City versus Manchester United, dog lover versus cat lover, custard versus ice cream, remain versus leave.

Despite the saying "opposites attract," the opposite is in fact true: similarities attract. The evidence proves there is a tendency for us to associate more with those who are like us rather than those who are not like us. Tajfel[18] defines this as our social identity; similarities give us a sense of belonging, pride and esteem. As we become older, the social constructs that humans created and contribute to leads to the narrowing of experiences – everybody around us is just like us and it feels positive – it is safe.

We sit in our bubbles and when somebody comes along who is different from us, our brains trigger an alert: there may be danger ahead. This way of thinking certainly was useful thousands of years ago; it got humans to where we are today, but the same way of thinking will not get humans to where we need to go tomorrow.

We must tread carefully to not stereotype people into social identities that they do not identify with, or which they identify with but less so, or where identities are used out of context.

> "Can you attend this meeting? The customer is a lesbian and I think you'll get on."

> "Are you free to meet them? It needs a women's touch."

Both of these statements were made to me during 2020 and both statements triggered a form of rage. Not because I do not identify as a lesbian or a woman, I do. But because when I am at work I am a professional, a consultant; not a woman, not a lesbian, but an experienced professional there to do a job. This is an example of how somebody's sense of identity can quite easily feel threatened.

The more varied and diverse experiences we have, the more neural pathways we develop, the more the 'status quo' image is broken down. This is a conscious choice that we can and must make. A human-centric workplace embraces everybody as unique individuals, firstly because it is the right thing to do and secondly because groups that include individuals who defy stereotypes and encourage collaboration reap the benefits. The more diversity, the more different experiences and perceptions, the more problem solving and innovation.

While considering difference, we must also note how people have different needs within the workplace environment, right down to where and when people work.

It may not come as a surprise to you when I say that I love working in an office, especially an office that I have played a part in cocreating; that sense of pride and the buzz seeing people working and knowing you have enabled them to come together, develop themselves and drive the organization. Being with colleagues, the belonging and connection, working together and innovating, the coffee machine chats and simply the divide and boundaries that the office provides between home and work.

However, I have also had times where I have disliked working in an office, not because of the physical workplace, but the culture. Arriving at a certain time, the expectation of leaving any personal matters at the door and being expected to perform, making energy available for others, knowing my boss could tap me on the shoulder at any point and the having to put headphones on to try and zone out to simply recharge my introverted self, the polite signal to others to please just leave me alone. One of my worst times in the workplace was when I sat next to an extrovert who spoke so loudly that the phone was probably not even necessary, but also they never, ever stopped talking.

During 2021, I started a new home-based role where the HQ is in Canada. I was nervous about the time zone differences, not having an office to see colleagues and build relationships, and in general, feeling disconnected from the organization. However, home-based roles do work but they require conscious effort and human-centric leadership underpinned by trust and communication.

There is no denying that I am a night owl; it is currently 2.42am. You may make some assumptions here that I am lacking in boundaries, overworked or have no life outside of work. But the truth is, I have a special relationship with work, a passion that goes way beyond the traditionally expected 9-to-5, and I always seem to get my best ideas at night.

I have tried tactics like writing the idea down ready for the morning or sending myself a quick email in the hope I can still fall asleep and remember my train of thought in the morning. But when I get an idea I feel alive, the cogs do not stop and, in truth, I have never really wanted them to. Choosing to ignore the idea not only stunts me as a human at work but could stunt the organization too.

The problem with this scenario has always been that the time I need to be in the office or working virtually has never taken this into account. This led to late nights, early mornings and consequently fuelling myself with coffee and living for the weekends. The vicious circle I found myself in led to stress, burnout and falling out of love with work and the organization. Becoming so frustrated at the very thing you are staying awake working on is a bizarre situation to find yourself in. The 9-to-5 in an office has never worked for me and I am not the only one. It was always a situation that I battled against and lost, not surprising really when it has taken a global pandemic for many organizations to see the value of hybrid working – more on this later.

I have a set of principles that I apply to my working life. It is these principles that I check in against during tough times:

→ Presenteeism is for fools; work when you are energized.
→ Listen to your gut. Always.
→ Never apologize for how you feel.
→ Do not question yourself.
→ Learning is never done.
→ Just do the right thing.
→ Remember your why.

It is following my principles, despite it being a challenge at times, that led me to deeply understand and value not just myself but those I lead. The principles give me a focus, something to reflect on, something to benchmark myself against.

Too often, leaders want to take the good of a team member and tell them the 'flaws' they need to work on; in reality, those 'flaws' often say more about the leader's unconscious bias or their lack of emotional intelligence than what it says about the team member.

Where we all individually perceive the behaviours of people will be somewhere on a continuum.

| | |
|---|---|
| Passionate | Emotional |
| Analytical | Pessimistic |
| Ownership | Defensive |
| Energizing | Distracting |
| Introverted | Shy |
| Extroverted | Mouthy |
| Assertive | Bossy |
| Determined | Feisty |
| Persuasive | Pushy |
| Dominant | Submissive |
| Self-sufficient | Dependant |
| Empathetic | Cold |
| Optimistic | Pessimistic |

Where an individual is on this continuum will vary between days, situations and for no apparent reason at all. Alongside this is that we all have our own perceptions and past experiences that feed our thoughts – humans are messy. We can all bring humanness to the workplace. For leaders, role modelling such behaviours is imperative for influence and impact:

→ Self-awareness – understand your own uniqueness and bring it to the party.

→ Acceptance – and the embracing of difference.

→ Curiosity – get to know, really know, the people you work with. What is important to them, what are their idiosyncrasies, hang-ups and dreams.

→ Gratitude – ensure that those around you know you value them and the reasons why.

→ Humility – be modest; nobody likes listening to a big head.

→ Listen – listen to hear and understand, not to reply.

→ Nurture humanness – give people permission to be more human.

→ Rebel conformity – be willing to stand out, to be your authentic self.

## GENERATIONS IN THE WORKPLACE

There are four generations in the workplace as of 2021: baby boomers (57–75 years old), generation X (41–56 years old) millennials (25–40 years old), and generation Z (9–24 years old). Between the four generations, there is a generation gap: differences in behaviour and outlook. Okay, so that is no big deal, I know people the same age as me who have quite different behaviours and outlooks, so why all the rhetoric?

The multigenerational workforce is not all what it seems – firstly, it is not negative, it is a strength. Secondly, the differences are not that different anyway. In fact, through assuming differences, we are treating people differently, making dangerous assumptions, dividing, and creating excuses, even shame, for certain behaviours.

For example, within the next five years millennials, the fastest-growing segment of the working population, will outnumber the boomers. Millennials, the generation of unique, entitled, overly emotional, easily offended, avocado-loving people – if you want to undermine them. Or if you want to see things differently, millennials are a generation of diverse, tech-savvy, curious, ambitious, purpose-driven, human-centric challengers who question authority, the norm, have high expectations and want to create a better world for everybody.

Millennials are the catalyst for workplace evolution, through purpose-driven brands, with flattened hierarchies and empathetic leadership, technologically driven with passion and new ways of living. The human-centric workplace is one that will be driven and powered by the millennial generation.

The human-centric workplace, a movement, will happen thanks to lots of small numbers of people pulling together to form a big number driving change as people choose their careers, aligning who they are with what they do.

To work together effectively, we must understand, respect and embrace each other. Each generation does have its own preferences and expectations, but there are lots of commonalities and with each generation comes different strengths and concerns. We must stop the tension, the eye rolling and undermining and see the workplace for what it is: a diverse set of people bringing lots of experiences and skills together for a common purpose.

# BE A REBEL,
# JOIN THE MOVEMENT

During a recent coffee with a previous boss, they said, "Well, you used to call things a spade, and now it is a shovel, so at least you've calmed down a little bit." I was not entirely sure whether I should be honoured or offended. They went on to say that honesty, integrity and common sense are all values missing from today's world that I should drive to keep alive.

I had a think and, as it should, it led to a conversation with my coach, who asked me to describe my approach to work and my career. I stuttered. I said I was values led. They asked, "Would you say you're a rebel?" Up to that point, the word 'rebel' would have been somebody who was a trouble-maker, a misfit, a round peg in a square hole.

There have been many times throughout my career where my values-led approach has been misinterpreted or labelled as a 'Northern thing.' I have shied away from it, wondering why I was coming across so differently for simply just being myself. I was made to think that I should fit into the world, change, be like other people, stop caus-ing trouble, play the game. A workplace rebel is somebody who resists the status quo. Albeit some will equate this to trouble, manage the rebels in your organization effectively and you will not look back. Rebels get sh*t done, bringing about change and transformation because they stick their heads above the parapet and use their energy for the things they believe in, telling the truth even when nobody wants to hear it. Good rebels fight the good fights.

As Megan Reitz and John Higgins[19] profoundly say, 'what you say or don't say can have life-defining consequences for yourself and those around you' – and it all comes down to T.R.U.T.H. – Trusting the value of your own opinion, evaluating the Risk of speaking up, Understanding the politics, owning the Titles and How to choose the right words at the right time in the right place.

Maybe you are thinking of somebody right now you think is a troublemaker. Next time you are feeling uncomfortable or threatened by somebody speaking out, ask yourself why. What buttons are they pressing? Do you know the whole picture? Do you know their drivers for speaking out?

There are righteous rebels and rotten rebels:

| RIGHTEOUS REBELS | ROTTEN REBELS |
| --- | --- |
| Strive to change 'the norm' | Break rules |
| Are optimistic that things can be changed | Are pessimistic about pretty much anything |
| Focus on the purpose | Focus on themselves |
| Are energizing | Are mood hoovers |
| Are problem solvers | Look to blame |
| Are curious | Are meddlesome |
| Create | Complain |
| Focus on the opportunities | Focus on the problems |
| Listen | Tell |
| Are passionate | Become angry |
| Have positive intentions | Are driven by revenge/deceit |

There are lots of famous rebels (that is probably not a coincidence):

Rosa Parks drove the Civil Rights Movement and was quoted as saying, "I would like to be remembered as a person who wanted to be free ... so other people would be also free."

Malala Yousafzai appeared on TV talking about how the Taliban banned girls from attending school. It took the Taliban just three days to lift the ban.

Florence Nightingale defied her parents to become a nurse. When the Crimean War broke out in 1853, Florence took 38 nurses to Turkey's military hospital, the first time women had been allowed to do so.

Marie Curie won two Nobel Peace Prizes and battled sexism throughout her entire career. She was quoted as saying, "I have frequently been questioned, especially by women, of how I could reconcile family life with a scientific career." Not only did Marie Curie's research contribute to the development of x-rays in surgery, but her tenacious spirit also set her apart from her male peers. During WWI she even helped equip ambulances with x-ray equipment, driving them herself to the front lines.

Nelson Mandela, the epitome of a rebel with a cause, headed the civil disobedience campaign against the unjust laws of the white segregationist regime in Africa, dedicating his life to fighting for equality.

Greta Thunberg started a global movement by skipping school for a day to demonstrate against climate change.

The common catchphrase among rebels in the workplace is that it is easier to seek forgiveness than to seek permission. For the righteous rebels, the rebels with good intentions, this approach can be worked with to build a level of discipline that is appropriate and prevents a total lack of respect from peers due to stubborn nonconformity.

Where this approach is being fuelled by a rotten rebel, the outcome will only ever result in toxicity.

The British Psychological Society concluded that being rebellious is unambiguously a key driver of creativity.[20]

> "... our study suggests that employee rebelliousness does not have to be a hazard for organizations. Instead, it has creative potential when employees pursue goals targeted at the attainment of success rather than the avoidance of failure."

Rebels can be quashed, asked to tone things down, made to feel like they are troublemakers, punished for taking risks and not following instructions. This leadership approach is driven by fear, the fear of risk. It takes a Human Leader to understand, drive, support, coach and give the person the psychological safety to be themselves, managing their skills and passion effectively; after all, some risks are worth taking.

## KEY TAKEAWAYS
## – SPEAK YOUR T.R.U.T.H

- A human-centric workplace is not a romanticized view of achieving perfection.
- Work forms part of an individual's identity.
- The most underused asset at work in the 21$^{st}$ century is being human.
- Human-centric workplaces are about integrity, values and not being a d*ck.
- No leader should ever make one of their team members feel like they should care less.
- Leaders must model the behaviours of the human-centric workplace; nobody is exempt.


## REFLECTIONS

- What does being human mean to you?
- When working, what parts of yourself do you leave behind?
- What energizes you?
- What time of the day are you most energized?
- What do you want to change right now?
- What principles do you live by?

# CHAPTER 2

# UNDERSTANDING
# THE BRAIN

Neuroscience provides a lens through which we can better understand ourselves and others, and when we understand, we can begin to change.

> "The human brain has 100 billion neurons, each neuron connected to 10,000 other neurons. Sitting on your shoulders is the most complicated object in the known universe."[21]

Although complex, understanding how our brains work will aid us all in not just understanding why workplaces need to be more human, but how as an individual you can help change the world of work for yourself and those around you.

By no means will this cover everything you can and need to know about the brain, but I will provide an overview of some key concepts and models as somebody who defines themselves as a human leader, not a neuroscientist.

Our brains have three main jobs: first, to manage our unconscious and automatic functions (heartbeat, breathing, digestion, body temperature); second, to manage our conscious functions (movement, gesturing, balance, posture, speech); and finally, thinking, emotions, behaviour and senses. Everything we do, think, feel and speak is controlled by the brain, and the brain's main goal is survival.

The three main functions occur in the three main parts of the brain: the cerebrum, cerebellum and brainstem. The cerebrum has four interdependent areas, the lobes: frontal, temporal, parietal and occipital, which are the outer layers of the brain. The cerebellum controls balance, fine motor skills and coordination. The brainstem controls breathing, arousal, consciousness, attention and concentration, heart rate and sleep cycles. The brainstem connects our brain to the spinal cord at the Medulla Oblongata. All information that relays between the body and the cerebrum and cerebellum, and vice versa, travels via the brainstem.

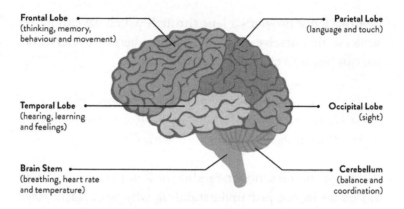

**Frontal Lobe**
(thinking, memory, behaviour and movement)

**Parietal Lobe**
(language and touch)

**Temporal Lobe**
(hearing, learning and feelings)

**Occipital Lobe**
(sight)

**Brain Stem**
(breathing, heart rate and temperature)

**Cerebellum**
(balance and coordination)

The limbic system is a complex set of structures found on the central underside of the cerebrum, comprising inner sections of the temporal lobes and the bottom of the frontal lobe. The limbic system encompasses the fornix, hippocampus, cingulate gyrus, amygdala, the parahippocampal gyrus and the thalamus.

## LIMBIC SYSTEM

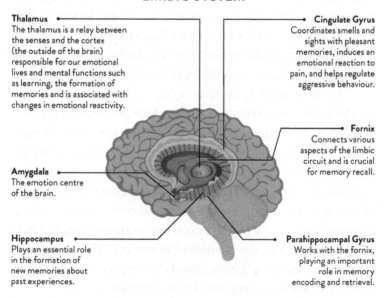

**Thalamus**
The thalamus is a relay between the senses and the cortex (the outside of the brain) responsible for our emotional lives and mental functions such as learning, the formation of memories and is associated with changes in emotional reactivity.

**Cingulate Gyrus**
Coordinates smells and sights with pleasant memories, induces an emotional reaction to pain, and helps regulate aggressive behaviour.

**Fornix**
Connects various aspects of the limbic circuit and is crucial for memory recall.

**Amygdala**
The emotion centre of the brain.

**Hippocampus**
Plays an essential role in the formation of new memories about past experiences.

**Parahippocampal Gyrus**
Works with the fornix, playing an important role in memory encoding and retrieval.

The limbic system is the reason that some physical things, such as eating birthday cake in the office, are pleasurable to us, and the reason workplace stress causes high blood pressure. The chemicals are not meant to be on and firing constantly, but surge when required to promote survival.

Our brains contain billions of brain cells (neurons). The cell bodies are grey in colour and known as 'grey matter' – they control all the brain's functions. The axons form connections, like wiring, between the brain cells, allowing communication across the brain network.

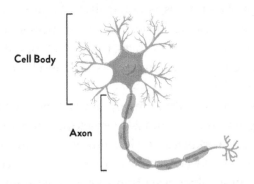

Cell Body

Axon

Although peak brain development occurs between ages 0–24 years, humans can improve brain function through-out life; hence the rise in the popularity of brain training. Neuroplasticity is the science behind growth mindset, the brain's ability to change and create new neural pathways to account for learning and acquisition of new experiences and the reorganization of functions from a damaged area of the brain to an undamaged area (rewiring of the brain).

Our ancestors survived, before schools and words, thanks to key chemicals within the brain released by the limbic system – adrenaline, the fight-or-flight chemical, which was especially useful to keep them alive when in danger from a sabretooth tiger way before risk assessments! Adrenaline is released when there are both imagined threats or actual threats.

The term 'adrenaline junkie' can be applied to the workplace: the taking of excessive risks, workaholic behaviour and/or the creation of high-stakes working cultures where leaders foster excessive competition between colleagues and/or act in a way that is deemed abusive.

Such adrenaline junkie behaviours can lead to workaholism, an unhealthy level of workplace competition and troubled relationships between colleagues. In a world that prioritizes work and values high status and financial rewards, careers offer a generous supply of adrenaline as people search to stave off feelings of emptiness, boredom, lack of power and anxiety.

Human-centric workplaces value interpersonal skills, the ability to cooperate with others, to enjoy a work life balance, and be driven by a clear purpose; as such, levels of adrenaline must be regulated.

Occupational health, employee assistance programmes, wellbeing action plans and 24/7 employee counselling helplines are all workplace staples; however, as much as they support an employee in times of need, they rarely address the root cause, which are often rooted in systemic working cultures that do not underpin employee wellbeing.

Human-centric workplaces intentionally create a culture of wellbeing, and the conditions enable and embrace people to generate more happy hormones. Our brains spurt happy chemicals that reward us with good feelings when we do something it perceives as good for our survival.[22] When happy chemicals flow, neurons connect and it feels good. The four happy chemicals relevant to creating human-centric workplaces are dopamine, serotonin, oxytocin and endorphins. Apart from a happy mood, they also give you energy and optimism, enable you to connect with those around you, give a higher focus and thus your drive, leadership and confidence at work are elevated.

Lieberman and Long[23] define dopamine chemicals as 'future oriented' and serotonin, oxytocin and endorphins as 'present oriented' – the 'here and now' chemicals. Dopamine and the here and now chemicals can work together but mostly counter each other. Here and now chemicals prompt the human brain to focus on the immediate world around us, and dopamine is suppressed; when dopamine is activated, our brains move to the future and the here and now chemicals are then suppressed.

Dopamine supports behaviour, emotion, cognition, pleasure and reward. Dopamine sparks before a task to obtain a reward; the purpose of dopamine is to make us act – it is our motivation and drive. When a human receives the reward, they will then set their sights on the next reward.

A human-centric workplace is a high dopamine environment, to create as such requires us to think holistically about all the facets that impact performance: ensuring individuals feel aligned to their roles, their colleagues and with the values and purpose of the organization. To get your body to increase healthy and sustained dopamine levels at work, you need to find out what rewards motivate you, link them to goals, and break down those goals to smaller short-term milestones, to trigger a reward and a dopamine high with each one.

While having a healthy dopamine surge to pursue a task is good, like adrenaline, dopamine addiction does occur within the workplace, and you can certainly have too much of a good thing! Signs of addiction include being busy, constantly moving onto the next task, difficulty remaining grounded in the here and now or issues concentrating during interactions with colleagues.

A leader with a dopamine addiction is never satisfied; they push their teams to achieve more and more, with less and less, setting unrealistic goals in pursuit of boosting their own greatness. Team members become overwhelmed and suffer from anxiety, stress, reduced engagement and increased burnout.

Leaders within the human-centric workplace benefit from regulated dopamine levels and draw on more stable emotions, which in return make them more stable and effective leaders who connect on a human level with those around them.

Endorphins are the body's natural pain reliever, stimulated by pain. Endorphins increase when you engage in reward-producing behaviour such as eating, laughing, exercise or physical intimacy and enable us to cope more effectively with stress and anxiety.

Oxytocin is the bonding chemical, the love hormone, stimulated by trust, touch, free expression of emotions such as laughter, smiling and deep listening. The stimulation leads to increased loyalty, trust, empathy and generosity within the workplace, enabling us to instigate, build and maintain satisfying relationships.

Oxytocin reduces stress levels and boosts security and contentment. To increase your oxytocin, take time to help, encourage, mentor or compliment people at the office. On the flip side, when you are separated from your herd or you feel like your trust has been betrayed, it feels like your survival is threatened and you no longer belong in that field. Spending time with your team beats the blues that come from working alone.

Serotonin supports appetite, arousal, mood and sleep. It boosts willpower, self-esteem, inner satisfaction, confidence and a sense of purpose alongside battling against cortisol – your stress hormone. A leader showing such traits as a strong purpose, confidence, self-worth and low stress is a leader who belongs in and drives a human-centric workplace.

Serotonin is reabsorbed quickly, which motivates people to seek another social advantage to stimulate more. A human can increase serotonin levels through nutrition, exercise, light, massage, medication, grounding themselves in the here and now and simply saying thank-you.

Within the workplace, reward and recognition are driven by dopamine and contentment driven by serotonin.

The chemicals affect how long the feeling lasts, the way it makes you feel, how it is achieved and the aftereffects. Lustig[24] sets out the differences between reward (driven by dopamine) and contentment (driven by serotonin):

→ Reward is short-lived. Contentment is longer term.
→ Reward is instinctive excitement. Contentment is calming.
→ Reward can be achieved with different substances that stimulate the reward centre of the brain. Contentment is achieved with deeds.
→ Reward occurs with the process of taking. Contentment is often generated through giving.
→ Reward when unchecked can lead us into misery, like addiction.

Aside from adrenaline and the four happy hormones, when we feel stressed, disappointed or feel threatened, cortisol is released, and alarms are sent that will connect to past pain. Cortisol is the body's main stress hormone that controls mood, motivation and fear. Unhappy chemicals connect neurons, so you learn about danger and once something causes you pain, your brain keeps trying to avoid it to protect yourself.

The brain seeks rewards and avoids pain using circuits built by past experiences; those circuits, built between ages 0–24 years, become the fast lane for your neurons. Unless we rebuild circuits (rewire our brains) the fast lane (old habits) will persist.[25] This is the equivalent of driving down a muddy dirt track, the familiar road you know, and then building alternative routes, smooth motorways, where you arrive quicker with fewer bumps in the road – the dirt track does not just go away, but you can choose to take the motorway more and more, and when you trust it, when you believe in it, it becomes your new route.

| AREA OF THE BRAIN | FUNCTION | BEHAVIOURS / ACTIONS | HOW TO EXERCISE (GROW) THE AREA |
|---|---|---|---|
| Frontal Lobe | The frontal lobes allow you to process and think about your emotions. Responses are rational rather than reactive. | Personality, behaviour, emotions. Judgment, planning, problem solving. Speech: speaking and writing. Body movement. Intelligence, concentration, and self-awareness. Personality, speaking, awareness of abilities and limitations, mental flexibility, inhibition of behaviour, problem solving. | Be optimistic.<br><br>Practice gratitude.<br><br>Volunteer.<br><br>Avoid autopilot, be curious and stretch your thinking. Learn something new.<br><br>Avoid information overload.<br><br>Watch less TV. |
| Parietal Lobe | The parietal lobe interprets language and words. Responses are intuitive.<br><br>The cingulate gyrus, within the limbic system, is located within this lobe. | Sense of touch, pain, temperature. Interprets signals from vision, hearing, motor, sensory and memory. Spatial and visual perception. | Sleep.<br><br>Brain-training activities such as Sudoku. |
| Temporal Lobe | The temporal lobe is key to preserving long-term memory and plays a role in processing emotions, language and hearing. Responses are reactive rather than rational.<br><br>The amygdala, hippocampus, parahippocampal, fornix, within the limbic system, are all located within this lobe. | When you sense danger is present, your amygdala wants to automatically activate the fight-or-flight response immediately. However, at the same time, your frontal lobes are processing the information to determine if danger really is present and the most logical response to it. Where threat is mild/moderate, the frontal lobes will override the amygdala. | Avoid drama.<br><br>Offer and receive physical contact.<br><br>Listen to music.<br><br>Nutrition and hydration.<br><br>Exercise.<br><br>Travel a different route home. |
| Occipital Lobe | The occipital lobe processes and interprets everything we see. The occipital lobe is also responsible for analysing content such as shapes, colours and movement, and for interpreting and drawing conclusions about the images we see. | Is crucial for processing what we see, where we see it and how we see it. | Brain-training activities using shapes.<br><br>Learn a new language.<br><br>Watch a 3D movie.<br><br>Meditation.<br><br>VR experiences.<br><br>Drive without GPS navigation. |

Human-centric workplaces ensure opportunities to produce happy chemicals, to increase happiness levels, and improve mental, physical and emotional wellbeing so people function at their optimum and bring and contribute their whole selves. Human-centric workplaces are where people want to be; they want to be part of the organization, they want to thrive as humans.

## HOW DOES OUR BRAIN AFFECT THE WAY WE LEAD?

Leaders inspire, influence and impact others in order to improve performance. There are many ways of leading, many of which belong in the past.

Old ways of leading – carrots and sticks – follows the pattern of a top-down approach to strategy: managers command and control and HR measures and acts. Money is used as an incentive and disciplinaries are used to ensure people toe the line. Leaders dictate to their subordinates, keep information to themselves and manipulate their people (intentionally or subconsciously) to follow them. Change happens to the people, not with the people, and innovations are scarce – "It is just the way things are done around here."

This type of management is still very much alive, unfortunately, despite it being relevant to the first industrial revolution work settings and all the evidence highlighting that first, people are not motivated by carrots or sticks, and second, this way of leading is not conducive to people thriving within a business – emotionally, physically or socially.

Human leadership is more in keeping with the Fourth Industrial Revolution, the revolution where boundaries between the physical and the digital are muddied, and with that comes transformative changes to the way we work and live. It is one that is more inclusive, with problem solving, innovation and continuous improvements happening at a team level. Employees are valued for their strengths, rather than punished for their weaknesses. Communication is the cornerstone to collaborative leadership and change happens with the people. Innovations are the norm; the culture embraces and encourages people to question how things are done. People are trusted, challenged, coached and built up to help them grow and continually evolve. Relationships are key to the being of the team and getting stuff done.

The brain is a social organ; we were born to connect. We must understand our people through deep listening, communication and getting to know them on a human-to-human deeper level. Through trusting, empowering, and recognizing the efforts made and feedback, your people will grow. A leader who does all of this, speaks from the heart, shows empathy, and communicates a clear vision, is a leader that people will climb mountains to follow.

The cultivation of a culture of teamwork will bond the team, drive trust and push them to dig deep when the chips are down, to ensure the success of the team and the organization, because they care.

Brains and hormones play a significant role in leadership. Leaders driven by endorphins and dopamine versus leaders driven by serotonin and oxytocin are a vastly different beast. Dopamine drives leaders to just get things done and endorphins drive short-lived happiness. Serotonin makes you feel good, not just about what you have accomplished, but what your team has accomplished, while oxytocin drives trust, safety and connection.

Like everything, we must keep hormones in balance. A balanced environment, in every sense, is a human-centric workplace. I have seen, worked with and experienced too many organizations high on endorphins and dopamine, fuelled by lavish office parties and extravagant bonuses leading to toxic leaders, excessive competition among team members and selfish mindsets.

These cultures cannot and will not change overnight; they are the organizations that people refer to when saying it is like trying to turn an oil tanker.

Office parties, social gatherings and away days are a common part of the workplace to drive morale, team spirit and relationships, all of which release endorphins.

Annual performance reviews, KPIs, training plans, salary increases, bonuses and awards, and highlighting of an individual's achievements all release dopamine.

Employee of the week, handwritten notes, a year-end team gathering to celebrate the team's performance and caring for your team during difficult times all release serotonin.

Random acts of kindness, buying your team's lunch, telling your team to log off early, office dogs – the small things that mean a lot, that let your people know you care for them and in return, they will climb mountains for you – all release oxytocin.

The best organizations I have worked with and experienced focus on the people, the building blocks of a true team environment to innovate and drive a clear purpose. There is gratitude, celebrations, small nuggets of kindness, teams pulling together to achieve, with laughter and friendship. These organizations are often more resilient and more agile; change is easier because the change it is not about the individual, it is about the team, the organization, and the purpose – there is a higher motive.

## EMOTIONAL INTELLIGENCE
## AND REGULATION

Human-centric workplaces can be severely impacted by emotional reactions and their rationality. That statement itself is a conflict, as humans do tend to separate emotions from rationality, with statements like "they are being too rational" or "they are being emotional," as if one precludes the other. But that is, of course, not the reality.

In fact, the balance of our emotions and rationality is the basis of emotional intelligence. Imagine if we were only rational; we would not feel joy, fear or anger as all decisions would have a justified reason. Likewise, imagine if we did not think and were only ever just showing emotion.

Let us imagine a situation that I absolutely dread: being stuck in a lift (an elevator for my American friends). If we were too rational, we would probably just shrug and take a seat until it was working again. If we were too emotional, we would probably head into deep panic, run around the lift, bump into the wall, and knock ourselves out cold. In fact, despite me imagining myself doing the latter, when the situation occurred, what happened was a sinking sick feeling in the pit of my stomach, some expletives, followed by pressing the emergency button and checking my phone for a signal. I was almost proud of the calmness, but I will not lie, after more than an hour the panic did raise its head!

The limbic system – the darn amygdala again – is responsible for that first moment of pause before it decides on fight or flight. The conflict wreaks havoc on our brains, but we are conditioned for survival; the response is instinctive. Cortisol and adrenaline flood our bodies to move us into action – Goleman[26] devised the phrase 'amygdala hijack' – where we cannot choose how we want to respond as our attention narrows as parts of our brain shut down and the survival instinct takes over. This is where our mind is say-ing "get out" or "how can they seriously be saying this?"

Through increasing emotional intelligence, we can understand and manage our emotions and use the infor-mation gathered to relieve stress, communicate, empathize and diffuse conflict.

The optimum spot where the brain functions best in terms of arousal is termed the 'window of tolerance'[27] and although this neuroscience is usually applied in therapeu-tic settings in relation to trauma, anxiety or other mental illness, it is relevant to the workplace. Our bodies and brains are with us when we work.

The fight-or-flight response is hyper-arousal and the freeze response is hypo-arousal. When you are coping well with the ups and downs of life – when your thoughts are rational, and your emotions are calm in response to daily stresses – you are said to be functioning within the 'win-dow of tolerance.' Essentially, it is the capacity to manage emotions when under stress.

To avoid the brain hijack by overriding the survival instinct with conscious awareness, we must remain grounded in the situation by being mindful. We can stay present despite intense emotion, regulate our nervous sys-tem through breath, and override the negative thoughts.

Through mindfulness, our body reaches equilibrium faster, restoring our thinking brain to listen and relate. Anger becomes clarity and sadness becomes compassion. The more we practice, the better we become – we rewire our brain and free ourselves from old ways of thinking.

People who suffer with PTSD, anxiety or stress show increased amygdala activation, which can trigger more frequent hijacks. Knowing your people is crucial in under-standing how they react, what triggers them, how to com-municate effectively and how you can support them.

Some workplace cultures wish for emotions to be left at the door. In the longer term, that culture breeds far and wide-reaching consequences. Faking or suppressing our feelings at work is tiring and damaging, Arlie Hochschild[28] coined the phrase 'emotional labour,' describing the façade we put up to hide what is going on underneath. The façade takes its toll, leaving you doubting your emotions, self-worth and feeling disconnected.

A human-centric workplace is one where people can express their feelings, be their true selves and receive unconditional positive regard from their peers and leaders. Judgment and shame creates defensiveness, acceptance fosters safety, honesty, and self-exploration. For example:

*'What the hell have you done?' = Shame, Judgment and Defensiveness.*

*"I can see you feel bad, shall we chat about what happened?' = Acceptance, Safety, Honesty and Self-Exploration.*

The term 'unconditional positive regard' was coined by Humanistic Psychologist, Carl Rogers,[29] defined as expressing empathy, support and acceptance to someone regardless of what they say or do – the power is in the human connection.

One study[30] showed that athletes who received unconditional positive regard were more motivated, confident, and resilient, whereas athletes who were criticized were less secure, less motivated and at risk of burnout.

Another study from 2018[31] found that employees who experienced unconditional positive regard from their colleagues felt valued which in turn enhanced motivation, performance and satisfaction as well as improving their sense of inclusion, belonging and collaboration, which increased workplace morale.

Note, it is crucial to avoid the mix up between unconditional positive regard with unconditional acceptance.

Human-centric workplaces' practicing values can express empathy but still implement disciplinary procedures where behaviours are harmful to the organization, its customers, or people.

I have experience working with one organization where their people interpreted the positive company values to mean there were no boundaries. When they were reminded there were boundaries, people soon vocalized their seemingly unwarranted discontent.

Human-Centric Workplaces believe and practice that everybody deserves to be treated as a fallible human being, regardless of whether we agree or like their actions or feelings.

## IMPACT AND INFLUENCE

Our brains strive to minimize danger and maximize reward. When our bodies are full of cortisol, we act out of fear; when our bodies are craving reward, dopamine is in the front seat, driving without wearing a seatbelt. To collaborate with and influence others, we must understand how their brains are working and what makes them tick.

The SCARF model[32] outlines the five factors that the brain monitors to determine whether we are in the danger state or the reward state:

→ S – Status – Where you think you are in relation to those around you.
→ C – Certainty – Ambiguity triggers the brain to think 'danger.'
→ A – Autonomy – A lack of control and choice raises cortisol levels.
→ R – Relatedness – The brain perceives people we have not connected with as a threat.

Once a handshake/smile/chat has taken place,
we have an oxytocin response. They become
'like us' instead of 'not like us.'
→ F – Fairness – A fair exchange activates dopamine;
an unfair response activates danger, cortisol.

I reflect on a manager I had in my early career (manager A).
They threatened me in all five elements of the SCARF model:

→ S – Their behaviour was consistently showing that
they were senior to me and that I was junior to them.
→ C – I had no clear expectations of what my job was,
and their day-to-day behaviour was erratic.
→ A – They micromanaged me.
→ R – The leadership style was transactional; I felt like
a cog in a machine.
→ F – I did not feel like my opinions mattered; I did not
feel supported.

I reflect on one of my more recent managers (manager B),
and wow, what a difference:

→ S – They increased my status, my confidence, by
telling me they learned from me and built me up
when I undersold myself.
→ C – They provided a vision and clear expectations of
how I fed into that vision.
→ A – I was trusted to make decisions, to control my
working day, my tasks.
→ R – We built a true human bond; there was trust,
protection and belonging.
→ F – I was treated fairly, I worked hard, worked longer
hours when required and in return was told to take
the time back.

When comparing manager A and manager B, there were some key differences for myself as a human at work, which I am sure most of you will resonate with in your own ways:

| AREA | WORKING *FOR* MANAGER A | WORKING *WITH* MANAGER B |
|---|---|---|
| Engagement | Disengaged | Engaged |
| Success | Stunted | Achieved more than expected |
| Motivation | Sunday evening 'urgh' | Sunday evening reflective journal and planning |
| Safety | Fear | Vulnerability embraced |
| Feedback | Defence | Gratitude |
| Happiness | Friday's at 5pm | Small wins every day |
| Confidence | Self-doubt and imposter phenomenon | Self-belief and imposter phenomenon challenged |
| Wellbeing | Anxiety and burnout | Boundaries |
| Trust | Questioned | So good it was never thought about or discussed |
| Teamwork | Competition | Belonging and togetherness |
| Laughter | To avoid crying | Every single day |
| Learning | Planned training to avoid not knowing anything | Mutual with the aim of growth |
| Mistakes | Fearful of and covered up | An opportunity to learn |
| Loyalty | Misplaced and dangerous | Valued and celebrated |
| Strategy | Dictated to | Inclusive – my thoughts and visions were listened to and incoporated. |

Alongside ability, motivation is a key contributor to performance. As the human race and the world has evolved, so has what motivates us and therefore leadership styles must evolve in line with the fact that, in today's world, people want to work in organizations where they feel their achievements are recognized and they are valued for the contributions they make. People want human leadership in a human-centric workplace (remembering that the workplace is both physical and virtual).

As a leader, to influence and impact, you must have a solid foundation of meeting your people's most basic needs. Although some may see this as an over-referenced concept, it is one that is still as relevant today as it was some 80 years ago when Maslow[33] highlighted that people are motivated to fulfil basic needs – the physiological, safety, love and belonging – before moving on to the more advanced needs of esteem and self-actualization. As leaders, we can unlock the potential in our people, but progress is often disrupted by the failure of meeting the most basic of needs.

Hertzberg[34] highlighted those basic needs as hygiene factors – salary, relationships, security, status, personal life, work conditions, company policy and administration and supervision. Hygiene factors are not motivators – they are the launch pad and, in the absence of them, the motivators such as personal growth, advancement, responsibility, work itself, achievement and recognition cannot be achieved.

While talking about hygiene factors, when advertising job roles: 20 holiday days, a competitive salary, breaks, parking, sick pay, the living wage, statutory pension, a bowl of fruit (aka 10 satsumas and a banana between three hundred people), a laptop, tea and coffee, an on-site canteen (a microwave and a toaster), dress down Friday and flexible working upon request – NONE of these are benefits, they are hygiene factors that should be a given.

For an individual, the Theory of Needs[35] highlights that we all have a dominant motivator – the need to achieve, the need to be affiliated or the need for power and how an individual behaves, and therefore how you lead them will be different depending on their dominant motivator.

People motivated by achievement want a challenge; they also want feedback to ensure they can consistently improve. People motivated by affiliation want to work on low-risk collaborative tasks, when giving praise provide it to them in private as they have little desire to stand out. People motivated by power want competition, end goals and to be in charge and when receiving feedback, they need directness and to see how what you are telling them will develop their career goals.

Vroom[36] built upon the theory of those before him and depicted: Motivational force = Expectancy x Instrumentality x Valence. Vroom distinguished between the effort people put in, their performance and the result. Closely aligned to the work of McClelland[37], Vroom identified that the result is valued differently by everyone – some may want a financial reward, others may want additional annual leave or just a simple thank you. We must get to know our team members and understand what motivates them on an individual level.

Herzberg[38] noticed that we can distinguish two types of factors influencing our attitude toward work: things that cause job satisfaction (intrinsic motivators) and factors that cause job dissatisfaction, such as hygiene factors not being met, leading to demotivation. It is important to recognize that deficiencies in some areas cannot be supplemented by elements of the opposite one.

If a hygiene factor has a negative effect (e.g. low pay) on overall motivation, we cannot improve it by boosting a factor from the intrinsic motivators group (e.g. assigning an ambitious task or giving a promotion). The key is that meeting hygiene factors does not increase the overall motivation; however, not satisfying them will strongly demotivate.

The lack of adequate salary strongly discourages, but the increase does not affect the long-term positive effect on motivation (it only reduces demotivation). By taking care of the hygiene factors, we create a space for factors increasing satisfaction. Everything we do within the workplace needs to be built upon strong foundations.

Porter and Lawler[39] used Vroom's theory as a foundation but departed from the traditional cause-and-effect view of motivation and considered that once the individual has completed the task, their motivation will drop if the intrinsic and extrinsic reward received did not match their expectations of the reward they have expected to receive.

Deci and Ryan[40] formed self-determination theory, which considered people's inherent growth tendencies and innate psychological needs, looking at what choices people make without any external influence or interference. They highlighted three basic psychological needs for health and wellbeing: autonomy, competence and relatedness.

Pink[41] argued that the carrot-and-stick approach to leadership is not relevant for today's workforce; instead, people want flexibility, to be creative, to learn, to receive feedback and to have a clear purpose – which is not purely financial. Pink, like Deci and Ryan, identified the three elements of motivation as autonomy, mastery and purpose.

This is not an exhaustive summary of all the motivational theories and models, and although there are views that are shared among each model, there is also conflict.

Using rewards and penalties will motivate in the short-term, say for one to three wage slips. So as a leader, do not put all your golden eggs in that one shiny basket; the golden eggs do not lead to an ongoing emotional connection with the company. In fact, if you give a team member too many golden eggs, it will commoditize what they have achieved and potentially demotivate them if they think they did it just for money.

I experienced this feeling after completing a large project, when I received little thanks but a large bonus. I know what motivates me, and I would have preferred a smaller bonus and a big thank you instead. I had deep connections to the purpose of the project; I wanted a human reaction, not a transactional one.

As a leader in a human-centric workplace, we must get to know our people and find out what motivates them and how they like to be rewarded – different approaches to motivation are necessary for different people and that is a fact that the human-centric workplace must embrace and act upon to enable our people to thrive. People leave managers more than they leave companies.

As poet Emily Dickinson highlighted in the 1800s, "Look after the little things and the big things will take care of themselves."

## BODY LANGUAGE

Body language, and the reading of nonverbal communications and feelings, are in our genes. In the absence of language, our cavemen ancestors needed to read body language and explorers and tribal leaders had to be able to read potential foes to know whether to trust or defend or attack.

Nonverbal reactions are controlled by the limbic brain – the amygdala processes physical and psychological stimuli to decide the threat level. It is the first part of the brain to receive emotional information and react to it.

Philosophers and scientists have connected human physical behaviour with meaning, mood and personality for thousands of years – notably as far back in time as Hippocrates, Aristotle and Charles Darwin. As humanity has evolved, so has our knowledge and understanding of the impact of body language. Fast[42] brought the subject of body language to the mainstream.

How we position our bodies, our closeness to and the space between us and other people, facial expressions, how our eyes move and focus, how we hold ourselves and interact with others is all through our body language.

Body language is a significant form of communication, universal around the globe, occurring consciously and unconsciously and often communicating the unsaid. Your body language, your position and movements, reveal your feelings to others. Other people's body language reveals their feelings to you.

There are some components to be aware of. Body language very much depends on context and the frequency and number of signals. There are also some minor differences culturally and with age and gender.

Somebody who spots their friend in the workplace – eyes widen, eyebrows raise, they smile and their face lights up. Somebody hearing feedback they do not like – they cross their legs and fold their arms, and they become defensive. Somebody feeling disappointed – shoulders come forward and the head lowers – they want the ground to swallow them up. Somebody who is surprised puts their hand on the base of their neck. Somebody being pressured to answer an unwelcome question compresses their lips – their lips are sealed.

There are some immediate practical things that we can all implement, such as mirroring and seating position.

Mirroring (limbic synchrony, if you want to be posh) is where we match our subtle body language signals.

Mirroring shows the other person that we are connected and engaged and assists in the creation and retention of rapport. Mirroring helps to get in tune with another person without words being required. Try it when speaking with somebody; match their pace of speaking, then slowly change that pace, and see if they mirror you, or change your seating position – sit forward, or lean back – and watch them mirror you. These small connections generate unconscious feelings of affirmation and feelings that the person is like you.

We use cues to drive behaviour. When you are in a rush and your very talkative neighbour collars you, after a few minutes, do your car keys come out of your pocket? Do you start walking? When a meeting is running over, how many of you click your pens in or close your laptop? Such stimuli are used to send nonverbal signals that require empathy, awareness and consciousness to interpret the meaning and the emotion of how somebody is feeling.

Within the workplace, as a leader, do you wait until a team member breaks down crying and goes off on sick leave before realizing that they were suffering with stress? Or are you looking for those cues, the small signals, to determine how they are feeling? Do they rush in each morning looking at the carpet, sit down and avoid eye contact? Do they skip lunch and work late? Are they withdrawn or overly sensitive?

Unfortunately, the small cues are often missed. As a leader, tune in to your people and get to know what their nonverbal cues are. What are their gestures? What is their posture? Are they mirroring you? Are they mirroring colleagues? Being connected, feeling seen and heard, is crucial for the human-centric workplace.

Seating position is an interesting one in the workplace and something that is often overlooked. Where we sit in relation to somebody else offers vast opportunities for improved relationships, communications and understanding.

| SEATING | IMPACT |
|---|---|
| Sitting opposite somebody | Can feel confrontational |
| A table between you | Can lead to the creation of tension |
| Chairs that are too close together | People may feel their personal space is being invaded |
| Sitting side-by-side on a sofa | Can feel a bit awkward in general; try to avoid side-by-side or opposite positions and aim for a 45-degree angle |
| Sitting too far apart | May affect trust and communications |
| Low sofas and coffee tables | Feel more relaxed so are good for informal conversations |
| For a group or team meeting, use a round table, rather than a square or rectangular table | This will avoid the creation of a head of the table and promote equality |
| If you wish to promote authority | Take a head-of-the-table position |

Our head, mouth and eyes are also significant with so many signals sent; just look at the amount of emojis on your phone – a beaming smile or a quivering lip. A nodding head, a shaking head, or a lowered head. We can tell if somebody is focused or not, whether they have a blank stare, a piercing look, or whether they are about to cry. When somebody is looking to their right, they are creating; when somebody is looking to their left, they are remembering – which is linked to the sides of the brain.

Limbs are used to signal openness or defensiveness; avoid crossing your arms when with a colleague and if crossing legs for comfort, try to have your knees pointing in their direction. Use hands to emphasize a point, greet people or wave goodbye and be aware of pen tapping as a sign of pressure.

Many signals indicate negative feelings, and there is a human tendency to see such signals as a weakness on the part of the person showing them. Remember that body language is about the situation, not the person. If you are picking up on negative signals, go deeper. Ask yourself what may be causing those feelings. They could be because 'you're the boss,' or tiredness, information overload, the temperature of the room, stress, illness or a disability. Avoid jumping to conclusions, and ask questions where in doubt.

A human-centric workplace understands body language and uses that understanding to gain better self-awareness and insight of our own and other people's feelings, embracing the emotion and the data that it provides for understanding and change.

## KEY TAKEAWAYS

- The brain can change with the creation of new neural pathways through learning and the acquisition of new experiences.
- Adrenaline drives the fight-or-flight chemical.
- The four happy chemicals relevant to creating human-centric workplaces are: dopamine, serotonin, oxytocin and endorphins.
- Cortisol is the stress hormone.
- Everything we do, think, feel and speak is controlled by the brain.
- As a leader, to influence and impact, you must have a solid foundation of meeting your people's most basic needs.
- Your body language, your position and movements, reveal your feelings to others. Other people's body language reveals their feelings to you.
- A human-centric workplace is one where people can express their feelings, be their true selves and receive unconditional positive regard from their peers and leaders.
- It is crucial to avoid the mix up between unconditional positive regard with unconditional acceptance,
- Understanding how our brains work will aid us all in not just understanding why workplaces need to be more human, but how as an individual you can help change the world of work for yourself and those around you.

# REFLECTIONS

- How do you challenge yourself?
- How are you currently recognized and rewarded?
- What motivators are in place to encourage positive connection and relationships with colleagues?
- Do you take regular breaks to rest your brain and reset?
- Do you regularly laugh at work?
- How physically active are you throughout the working day?
- What small cues are you / your colleagues giving off?
- Are you able to express your feelings at work without feeling shamed?
- What seating position do you take up when joining a meeting with peers? - does that differ when you join a meeting with people you manage?
- How does your mood effect how human you are within the workplace?

# CHAPTER 3

# ORGANIZATIONAL
# **CULTURE**

Every organization has its own culture, ethereal and floating around, influencing how stuff happens, what stories are told, who fits in and who does not. There are written and unwritten behaviours and attitudes that influence the way people think, act and are; the why and the way that sh*t gets done:

→ By whom?
→ At what speed?
→ Are they seeking permission or asking for forgiveness?
→ Are they powered by initiative or consumed by bureaucracy?
→ What motivates them and how are they rewarded?
→ How do they behave when nobody is watching?
→ Are people smiling/laughing or withdrawn and stressed?
→ What is the hierarchy? What does it look and feel like?
→ Is performance measured by outcomes or time?
→ Do teams compete and squirrel away knowledge or do they collaborate and share?
→ Is it all about 'me' or 'we'?
→ What stories are told about the organization?
→ How is strategy influenced, set and acted upon?
→ What does the space look and feel like?

Company values and employee perks do not define company culture. Many organizations fall into the trap of offering amazing swag bags to new recruits to highlight how good their culture is but then fail to deliver – do not be that organization. Values guide culture; perks should be a by-product of intentional actions to create an organization that people want to work for.

Every organization combines a mix of four different types of organizational culture, which are represented within a competing values framework.[43]

The framework highlights how the four cultures compete within four parameters: internal focus and integration versus external focus and differentiation, and stability and control versus flexibility and discretion. Based on these parameters, the framework breaks organizational cultures into four distinct quadrants or cultural types. The dynamic, entrepreneurial create culture (Adhocracy), the people-oriented, friendly collaborate culture (Clan), the process-oriented, structured control culture (Hierarchy), the results-oriented, competitive compete culture (Market):

| | THE ADHOCRACY CULTURE | THE CLAN CULTURE | THE HIERARCHY CULTURE | THE MARKET CULTURE |
|---|---|---|---|---|
| The culture is grounded in ... | Energy | Collaboration | Structure and control | Competition and results |
| Employees are ... | Creative | One big family | Controlled, formal and uniformed | Goal oriented |
| The leader's approach is ... | Entrepreneurial and innovative | Facilitating and mentoring | Organized coordination and monitoring | Tough and demanding |
| The organization is held together by ... | Experimentation and risk taking | Traditions and commitments | Strict institutional procedures | The goal of beating rivals |
| The main values are rooted in ... | Individual ingenuity, freedom and agility | Teamwork, communication, and consensus | Efficiency, predictability, consistency | Market share and profitability |
| The downsides are ... | Lots of risks and potential competition between employees as they try to come up with the next big thing | Difficult to maintain as the organization grows | A lack of creativity and innovation, slow to adapt to change and people left feeling they do not have a voice | Purpose and employee engagement is lacking as the culture feels transactional |

| | THE ADHOCRACY CULTURE | THE CLAN CULTURE | THE HIERARCHY CULTURE | THE MARKET CULTURE |
|---|---|---|---|---|
| Where you will find it most ... | Large tech companies | Start-ups, smaller organizations, healthcare, education, not-for-profits | Banking and insurance, customer service-led organizations, the military or medicine | Large companies that are already market leaders |
| What would this work like in a human-centric workplace? | Creative and energetic. The psychological safety to take risks. Agility and freedom | Collaboration, communication, teamwork, mentoring | Clarity and efficiency to benefit the end user | The purpose of the organization fuels the reason for growth |

Defining any one culture is difficult. Departments within an organization will exhibit subdominant traits that are relevant to their areas; for example, finance may have a mainly hierarchy culture, while web development may be more adhocracy. The four cultural types align with the biological determined drives in the brain: the need to bond, to learn, to acquire and to defend – what makes us human. The mix will be unequal and there will almost certainly always be a dominant type and that dominance will be situational. Human-centric workplaces manage the competition between cultures and tap into each value set at the right time.

One of my childhood games, the labyrinth – a wooden game where you navigate a ball through a maze without it falling into a hole – very much reminds me of organizational culture. We all start out at the same place, but what we bounce off, what traps we fall into and the direction we take is determined by us. The end goal is that shared company mission that we all strive toward.

The path we take is certainly guided, but it will not be the same path that everybody takes; we each have our own values, perceptions and experiences. Demographics such as age and education of organizational members can lead to different values of each cultural dimension that individuals perceive.[44] Cooke and Rousseau[45] also report intra-organizational differences in behavioural norms across hierarchical levels. Thus, occupational values that individuals acquired during formal education may result in subcultures within an organization.

> "Culture is like the wind. It is invisible, yet its effect can be seen and felt. When it is blowing in your direction, it makes for smooth sailing. When it is blowing against you, everything is more difficult."[46]

Over recent years, culture has been highlighted as being a trend driven by the younger generations. However, do not be deceived as culture, connectedness and tribal belonging dates to the Palaeolithic Age (2.5 million years ago), where tribes typically consisted of around 25 hunter-gatherers who lived, worked and migrated together. The study of early humans often focuses on biological evolution and natural selection. However, it is equally important to focus on sociocultural evolution, the ways in which early human societies created culture.

> "Cultures evolved and developed in specific environmental contexts, enabling their communities to not only survive but to thrive in unique and dynamic ways ... cultural creativity rather than physical transformation became the central way humans coped with the demands of nature."[47]

There is an abundance of research on workplace culture; there is also an abundance of chatter in day-to-day life that relates to culture. One of my friends recently declared that her team had to chip in to buy a fridge for a staff room for their milk; another tells me of the glaring looks she receives when she leaves her workplace to collect her child from school; and another tells me how she is not allowed to contact anybody above their manager without asking their manager first.

The juxtaposition are the friends who tell me of their experiences where their leader contacts them to see how they are and say thank you, where they are sent flowers because they felt unwell and where CEOs meet with new recruits to get to know them as people.

So, what is a good organizational culture? Well there is not an empircally good or bad culture per se; it is down to each individuals experiences, values, expectations, and the behaviours of their immediate boss often determines how they experience company culture.

Aristotle looked across sciences and arts to define what good meant. He argued that in medicine it is good to be healthy. In strategy, it is good to win. In music, it is to play well. He argued that we can recognize the highest good because we do everything else for its sake.

In true philosophers' style, Aristotle went on to question the sake of those things and found he could always find another reason. For example, it was good to be healthy because he could live a fuller life, it was good to play music well as people would then listen and he would become famous. And again, he asked why enjoying a fuller life would be a good thing and why he wanted people to listen to his music. In the end, Aristotle concluded that all paths lead to happiness and, therefore, the highest good was a happy life.

Cultures are not defined by one big event; culture is defined by culminative small events and behaviours over time. Culture should not feel like you are trying to herd cats wearing roller skates, it should just flow.

For far too long, organizations have been feeding the rhetoric that the customer is always right and comes first.

Whoever started that rumour clearly has never worked in a customer-facing role! Maybe what we should have been saying is that through putting our people first, they will look after the customers in the right way, whether they are right or wrong.

My workplace, good and bad, will be different from your good and bad, but there is one key trait that will determine whether an organizational culture is good or not. A good culture is where people are happy. When people are happy, they thrive; when happy people thrive, so will your business.

| |  |  |
|---|---|---|
| The approach | People-centric. Teams, community, and friends. You feel valued as a person. | Organization/finances-centric. Cliques, departments, and colleagues. You feel like a cog in a machine. |
| Innovation | Big ideas are welcomed and will spark creativity from others. People are comfortable taking measured risks and making mistakes. | Things become stale; any snippet of an idea is quashed as it is "not what we do around here." No risk taking; they are not prepared to be humiliated. |
| Purpose | People are connected to the purpose, and it motivates them to succeed. | Staff are more connected to their pay packet and bonus. |
| Customers | People strive to keep customers happy and ensure they return. Good innovation, customer service and price. | Staff see customers as the bane of their lives and are relieved when they say they will not be back. Lagging competitors, unhappy customers and pricing is not in line with the market. |
| Engagement | People put in their best work. It is lovely to work there. A sense of pride and enthusiasm for the organization. Morale is high. | Staff turn up, sometimes. They feel the Sunday evening fear. It is just somewhere you work. Is it Friday yet? What's morale? |
| Trust | People are trusted to do what they think is best. People have a voice and speak up. | Staff are questioned over every move. People head to Glassdoor to have a voice. |
| Wellbeing | People are well and thriving. | People are ill, stressed and surviving. |
| Storytelling | Stories are told to engage and inspire. | There is toxic gossiping. |

| |  |  |
|---|---|---|
| Collaboration | It is all about 'we.' | It is all about 'me.' |
| Feedback | Clear expectations and open communication. Regular feedback, positive and negative. Transparency. | Bullying and wearing down. Public ridiculing and annual reviews. Insecurity and uncertainty. |
| Success | Wins are celebrated. Reward and recognition are in line with efforts. | Wins are used to ridicule others. Rewards and recognition are in line with output, and the best way to get what you want is to threaten that you are leaving the organization. |
| Leadership | Leaders are visible, accessible and approachable. Leaders lead by example. | You are told to only speak to your direct manager. Managers can do and say what they like, they are managers. |
| The workplace | The physical workspace is invested in to enable people to thrive. | The physical workspace looks like it hasn't been touched since the 60s. |
| Career development | Clear routes of progress to aspire to. Agreed and discussed targets for accountability and responsibility. Continued development of people. Nurturing. Internal progression and lower-than-average turnover rates. Learning is never done. | You must play golf with the boss. Finger pointing and blame. Annual tick boxes. Stunting. Signs of stagnation with 'life timers' and the ambitious and developing people choosing to leave to progress themselves. Annual tick boxes – how many manual handling courses do people need to do to use a phone? |
| Equality | Equality, inclusion and diversity. Respect, fair treatment, and equal opportunities. | Everybody looks, talks, sounds and thinks the same. Managers, and the friends of the managers, know how to play the game and they play it well. |
| Recruitment | Hire for culture fit. | Hire solely because of their skills. |
| Ways of working | Reasonable and flexible working schedules. Sharing of information and collaboration – one team. | Juggling parenting around an 8am meeting the boss insisted on, like they do every single day. Politics and internal conflicts. |
| Communications | Timely, honest, and transparent communication. | Gossip, rumours and secrecy. |

We talk about culture as if it is something that evolves naturally within an organization. Good organizational cultures, where people thrive, take conscious and consistent effort, time and patience. They take a healthy nudge to avoid the path of least resistance – the toxic workplace.

In thermodynamics, entropy tells us that systems tend to gradually decline into disorder. This principle can be applied to organizations – without the healthy nudges toward positive cultures, you can expect the culture to crumble into anarchy.

As such, the mantra is often that culture starts at the top and therefore to affect meaningful change, you need executive buy-in. However, the culture in which the executive intends to create is only half of the puzzle.

The systems theory of management states that each business is a system, much like a living organism, with numerous things going on to keep the operation rolling along. A business is not just its CEO, like a person is not just a brain. A person needs other organs and other key features to live. A business needs more than just a CEO to thrive.[48] A human-centric workplace recognizes the impact and value of the people who comprise the organization.

It is the organization of a business that defines how it is structured and how that structure helps meet the purpose and objectives. People working together (or not) to achieve a common (or not so common) goal.

The top-down intended culture drives organizational values, hierarchy, competitive advantage, creativity and innovation. What the business does and how people perform will drive actual culture: morale, belonging, networks and relationships, performance, customer service and financial performance.

The intended culture + the people, tasks and behaviours = the actual culture.

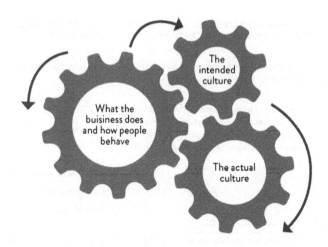

Delegating and compartmentalising culture is a thing of the past, no longer is it just the CEO telling HR how they want the culture of the organization to be delivered. Culture is everybody's responsibility. Every person in an organization has a role to play, a function and it flows through the organization.

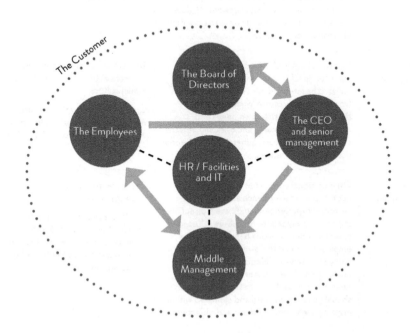

| JOB ROLE | THEIR RESPONSIBILITIES AND IMPACT ON ORGANIZATIONAL CULTURE | IN PRACTICE THIS LOOKS LIKE … |
| --- | --- | --- |
| The Board of Directors | To guide and align the culture to business goals and the stakeholders' demands. | A regular agenda item to discuss culture. |
| The CEO and senior management | To define and bring the culture to life through actions, objectives, and strategies, ensuring the organizational design and the operations support the delivery of the intended culture. | Ongoing conversations and SWOT analysis. Reviewing survey feedback (employees and customer). Ensuring new hires in senior roles meet culture leadership requirements. Communication. Role Modelling. |
| HR, Facilities and IT | The golden triangle focuses on designing the employee experiences which interpret and reinforce the intended culture, from culture decks and performance management to training programs and the physical spaces and technology which enable people to thrive. | Ensuring the day-to-day employee experience is aligned to the intended culture through tools and the environment. Application of the culture building objectives and strategies in the context of their function. Communication. Role Modelling. |
| Middle management | To deliver those experiences and culture-building strategies. They are the voice and role models of the organization downward and the voice of the people upward. Middle management are a crucial cog in the creation of organizational culture. | |
| The Employees | Firstly, to loop back round with providing input to the CEO and senior management on how the intended culture aligns or differs from the actual culture, what is best for the customer and their own needs and expectations. Secondly, and critically, it is the employees who create, adhere to, and enforce the norms and routines. | To feedback on the alignment/differences between intended and actual culture. Create the organizational culture norms and behaviours, role modelling and calling out behaviours which do not adhere. |
| The Customer | Organizational culture has a direct impact upon customer experience and therefore customer experience should have a direct impact upon organizational culture. Customer-centric cultures produce happy customers, employees should feel empowered to take charge and solve problems and be measured on doing so. Where customers are unhappy, feedback provided back to the organization should be taken onboard and captured within organizational culture drivers and objectives. | Feedback in relation to satisfaction and experience. Use leverage as a customer to demand better e.g. look at how many customers now refuse to shop with certain brands because of their publicized culture! |

In a strong organizational culture, employees know how the organization wants them to respond to any given situation; the response would be in line with the communicated and practiced company values, and they carry out tasks in a way that they believe is fitting, and the organization is successful as a result. Ultimately, they are self-perpetuating cogs; a web of interconnected human behaviours – the way that sh\*t gets done, the attitude of those doing it and the unspoken rules that develop.

Interrelated with organizational culture (the values) is the culture climate (the observable). Andy Swann[49] says that culture is an observable consequence of the connection between a business and its people – an indicator of how an organization is functioning.

The biggest challenge I have seen is not whether an organization has a good or bad culture, but whether the core values and behaviours are consistent across leadership, departments and teams.

Bureaucracy, the disease of an organization, results in uninspiring toxic wasteland. Gary Hamel[50] gives a lucid description of how many easily fall into the trap:

"Strategy gets set at the top. Power trickles down. Big leaders appoint little leaders. Individuals compete for promotion. Compensation correlates with rank. Tasks are assigned. Managers assess performance. Rules tightly circumscribe discretion."

The troubling part is how the vast majority of large-scale organizations (and most of the smaller organizations too) are operating. In a world of exponential technology, agility and humanness, organizations cannot afford to operate as they have always operated, they cannot afford for executives to dodge change, to lead through command, control and hierarchy and for creativity, innovation and contributions to run down the drain.

The inability to think differently, to see varying views of opinion and to evolve are all energy hoovers to those who want to be unlocked to thrive.

"Organizations grossly underutilize their human potential because they are overly focused on structure, rules, procedures, processes and extrinsic rewards. While these are all important in organizing work and moving organizations toward their goals, they are only important so long as they support and guide human potential – and definitely do not hinder it."[51]

I have experienced working with excellent teams in poor organizational cultures and poor teams in excellent organizational cultures. With an excellent team in a poor culture, I can only compare it to the feeling of trying to push treacle up a mountain with a fork when the rest of the organization wants the treacle to flow down the mountain; you are the minority, and it is draining ... soul destroying, even. With a poor team in an excellent culture, it feels much easier overall; the team stands out and etiquette wins, the majority wins.

A human-centric workplace is not only about a new approach, but also about challenging and letting go. Challenging shared common beliefs and letting go of old patterns that no longer serve a purpose. Being aware of and avoiding unnecessary process, complexity, levels of decision-making and hierarchy, knowing that it is not only one of the biggest frustrations experienced by people within the world of work, but it is bad for business. The human-centric workplace is a movement against bureaucracy. A movement that will not happen in small numbers, but lots of small numbers pulling together to form a big number.

# MEASURING ORGANIZATIONAL CULTURE

An organization needs the ability to state that the behaviour of their employees is in line with intended culture and core values. To maintain the intended culture, organizations need the ability to detect behaviours before they become a problem. There are some difficulties here; firstly, there is no scientific unit or universal methodology (yet) for measuring the culture of a group of individuals. Secondly, there is not an empirically right or wrong culture. Lastly, culture performance is not a constant, moving and evolving over time in line with organizational growth, recruitment and retention, leadership, strategy, customer needs and forces such as technological advances. And yet, measuring culture is necessity to determine whether that can determine the dominant culture type, how strong it is, the differences between the culture you have and the culture you want and where your people feel pain and where they would like to see changes.

Such measurements use employee feedback and often come in the form of a moment-in-time survey, which comes with flaws as they rely on the employee to have self-awareness of how they and others behave. This brings challenges with perceptions, unconscious bias and mood. There are various other ways used to collate data: pulse surveys, focus groups, one-to-ones and ethnographic studies. A human-centric workplace uses a blend and ensures the right culture metrics are in place, through collating both qualitative and quantitative data through a three-phased approach:

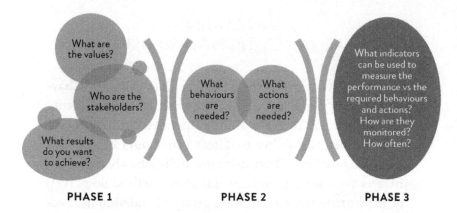

**PHASE 1**          **PHASE 2**          **PHASE 3**

Data and the sources are all crucial for the collation of cultural performance metrics; analytics and dashboards are crucial for the interpretation of the data. There are many indicators of how successful the organizational culture is or is not, with some of the indicators the challenge is to make what is naturally subjective as objective as possible, while accepting that there is almost always a need for qualitative judgment. The data collection often straddles nine cultural indicators.

An interesting study[52] used big data processing to look at what email, Slack and Glassdoor reveal about an organizations culture. They examined the diversity of thoughts, ideas and meaning expressed by team members and then measured whether it was beneficial or detrimental to team performance. They analysed how employees talk about their organizations' culture in anonymous reviews to examine the effects of cultural diversity on organizational efficiency and innovation.

Too often within the workplace world, data is collected and leaves the user with the "so what?" question, and by the time they have interpreted the data (through their own lens), it is out of date. To avoid the proverbial situation where data is collected and then filed and never looked at again, the data needs to be meaningful and clearly presented to the end users. This is where the importance of bespoke data dashboards comes in. Dynamic data, which is evolving, meaningful and extrapolating out into the future – what does the data tell you about what is going to happen next? It is this data that should be used to make informed decisions about the organization.

> "If you focus on results, you will never change. If you focus on change, you will get results." (Jack Dixon, Welsh Rugby Union Player).

It is time for change. It is time for human-centric organizational cultures; cultures where people thrive. Cultures where there are shared values, beliefs, assumptions, symbols, rituals, attitudes and behaviours possessed by a group of employees, lived and breathed by leadership and underpinned across space, technology and process.

## CULTURE INDICATOR #1:
## ENGAGEMENT

We all want to do work that matters, yet I still experience, see and hear about all the organizations that still think that purely paying people a wage is enough to engage them in being a vehicle to meeting the organization's goals, often financial.

Financial reward is not a long-term deep and impactful motivator that builds loyalty to the organization, to the team or to the organization's purpose. Financial reward alone creates transactional relationships.

**COMPANY A:**

= £40,000 + Company Car = Transactional Relationship

**COMPANY B:**

= £40,000 + Company Car + Purpose + A Human-Centric Workplace = True Connections

Company B is a culture where people thrive; they will dig deep when the chips are down because of the relationships, connections and the two-way bond that exists.

To capture employee engagement, surveys are the most widely used indicator but the value they bring can often be polarized. Using an independent survey will prevent issues with unconscious bias and leading questions and ensure people are honest. Equally as important is ensuring the analysis has not been massaged. In analysing the results of the survey, it would also be useful to triangulate the message with other indicators such as staff turnover, exit interviews, Glassdoor reviews and absenteeism rates.

Gallup found that 60% of employees do not know what their organization stands for. If so many people are spending time doing something without knowing why, it is no wonder engagement is so low. And 85% of employees worldwide are not engaged or are actively disengaged in their jobs.[53] There is a whole load of talent out there and our poor and medieval approaches to work are leaving our talented people frustrated, worn down and quite frankly giving up hope.

Gallup's global surveys find that just 15% are currently engaged at work – that is, psychologically invested in their job and motivated to be highly productive. Two-thirds worldwide (67%) are not engaged, putting in time but little discretionary effort at work, and 18% are actively disengaged – openly resentful that their workplace needs are not being met.

Then there is mental health illness and work-related stress that are at an all-time high and people are happy to leave their job and take a pay cut for a job that is more flexible.

What I find alarming about these statistics is that an organization's biggest asset, yet largest cost, is people. An engaged person is an asset delivering value; they will climb mountains for you. A disengaged person is a cost, an energy sap to those around them, and an actively disengaged person is potentially causing havoc.

| | | |
|---|---|---|
| Opportunities to learn and grow | The wrong type/level of training | No training |
| Boundaries that align to life outside of work | Overworked | Burnout |
| Trust and autonomy | Directed to | Controlled and distrusted |
| Alignment of the organization's purpose, values and behaviours | A mismatch of what the organization stands for and the way leadership behaves | Leaders and individuals are fuelling a toxic workplace culture |
| Friends at work and a sense of belonging | 'I' instead of 'we' culture. Feeling like a square peg in a round hole | Cliques and gossip |
| A human-centric culture that enables people to thrive | Actions that may seem like the organization is not putting people first | A culture of competitiveness and toxicity driven by financials |
| Sufficient challenge and job satisfaction | Monotony | Excessive workloads and pressure or no challenge at all |
| Effective, timely communication | Inaccurate communication | A lack of transparency |
| Pay/benefits | A change to pay/benefits | Underpaid versus market averages |
| Recognition and gratitude | No feedback | They feel invisible |
| Leaders who care | Poor leadership | Toxic leadership |
| Tools and technology to enable | A lack of tools and resources | Inefficient ways of working that lead to frustration |

We know organizations are capturing the voice of the people given the number of surveys, statistics and white papers bandied around, yet engagement across the board continues to lag.

If people are joining your organization, full of enthusiasm, energy and ideas and then leaving to join your competitor when they are feeling drained, frustrated and like they have been involved in an abusive relationship – what happened? Yes, okay, a small percentage might be down to the individuals, but seriously, too many organizations are kidding themselves and have been for far too long.

How are we making such a hash of it? is it simply that organizations are not listening? I am optimistic in thinking that maybe many just do not know where to start and therefore I am hopeful that *The Human-Centric Workplace* can be of inspiration it is time to live up to some truths, no matter how painful they may feel.

## CULTURE INDICATOR #2: HAPPINESS AND WELLBEING

Work is an important aspect of an individual's life, not only economically, but work meets the needs for psychological and social fulfilment. For many, work is also their purpose. A key driver for, and an outcome of, organizational culture is the wellbeing of people, with happiness being one of the most valued and pursued goals of an organization. For some companies, physical health and safety is a critical indicator; for others, it will be the incidence of mental health problems.

For true wellbeing, for people to thrive at work and in life, the varying aspects of wellbeing must be aligned and sustained, the: physical, emotional, financial, spiritual and the psychological.

Natasha Wallace[54] pinpoints that Conscious Leadership is the foundation for wellbeing and homes in on wellbeing in the sense of ensuring our intrinsic needs as humans are met – the need for relationships, the need for meaning, and for humans to have the ability to take better care of our own mental health. Natasha argues that where leaders are conscious of their own needs and others, and they know how to take care of them, they create environments that people want to be part of – I simply cannot agree more.

A Workplace that is full of leaders who are highly strung, snappy, and tense because they are under too much pressure, working too many hours, suffering from burnout, and not aware of the vibes they are giving off – no, that is not a workplace that anybody wants to be part of, never mind one where people can thrive.

Happiness is subjective and often fleeting; in the moment we can feel happy but still not be well. Where pieces of the workplace puzzle combine to make us feel unhappy, this will soon have a negative effect on wellbeing. On the flipside, where people repeatedly feel positive emotions – happiness at work, resilience builds, which in turn has a positive effect on our longer-term wellbeing and therefore performance and success.

Lyubomirsky[55] captures happiness as "the experience of joy, contentment or positive well-being, combined with a sense that one's life is good, meaningful, and worthwhile'." Happiness is individual to a person – we all want to be happy, organizations want us to be happy, the whole world just wants to be happy.

People often correlate happiness with money, materialistic items and status. Myers and Diener[56] compared income and happiness and found that there was no correlation where democracy, safety, equality and education were considered. Not only that, but Jebb[57] found that happiness peaks at an income of $100,000 and begins to reverse above $250,000.

During 2021, Finland was ranked 'happiest country' for the fourth time in a row.[58] The ranking was determined with measures that included asking countries to rate their own happiness; life expectancy, freedom to make life choices, social support, gross domestic product (GDP) and the levels of corruption were also factored in.

When reviewing the happiness ranking alongside hours worked, average salary, time spent on leisure, quality of support networks and gender equality, the element of consistency shone through the results. The more consistent a country was across various elements, the happier their people were. Happiness leads to longer lives, better relationships, more friends and success.

[59]

| Country | 2021 Happiest Country Rank | Average working week | Employees who worked over 50 hours/week | Average annual wages | Time devoted to leisure and personal care per day | Community: quality of support network | Gender equality in employment |
|---|---|---|---|---|---|---|---|
| Finland | 1 | 39.3 hours | 3.8% | $44,111 | 15.2 hours | 95% | 67.1% |
| Denmark | 2 | 37.2 hours | 2.3% | $55,253 | 15.9 hours | 95% | 62.3% |
| Switzerland | 3 | 40.5 hours | 0.4% | $64,109 | 15.1 hours | 93% | 68.2% |
| Iceland | 4 | 43.3 hours | 15.1% | $66,504 | 14.1 hours | 98% | 81% |
| Netherlands | 5 | 37.3 hours | 0.4% | $54,262 | 16.1 hours | 91% | 64.8% |
| Norway | 6 | 38.0 hours | 2.9% | $50,956 | 15.6 hours | 94% | 64.2% |
| Canada | 7 | 39.1 hours | 3.7% | $54,630 | 14.6 hours | 93% | 65.7% |
| USA | 14 | 41.5 hours | 11.1% | $63,093 | 14.4 hours | 93% | 63.1% |
| UK | 18 | 41.8 hours | 12.2% | $44,770 | 14.9 hours | 94% | 63.5% |

The Nordic countries are consistently ranked among the happiest in the world. From 2013 until 2021, each year the World Happiness Report (WHR) has published its annual ranking of countries, the five Nordic countries – Finland, Denmark, Norway, Sweden and Iceland – have all featured in the top ten.

Even though the Nordic countries are characterized by indicators of good society such as well-functioning democracy, generous and effective social welfare benefits, low levels of crime and corruption, and satisfied citizens who feel free and trust each other and governmental institutions, there is also another aspect to consider – mindset.

Csikszentmihalyi[60] highlighted that a person can make themselves happy or miserable despite what is happening on the outside, by rearranging the contents in the inside, within the conscious mind.

The Denmark practice of Hygge: "Hygge means creating a warm atmosphere and enjoying the good things in life with good people. The warm glow of candlelight is hygge. Cosying up with a loved one for a movie – that's hygge, too."[61] Hygge is also strongly associated with the Nordic countries of Sweden, Norway, Finland and Iceland. Norway names the cosy feeling and finding joy in the little things as 'Koselig,' and Sweden names the simple balance as 'Lagom.' The Netherlands practice 'Gezelligheid' – which is all about friendliness, togetherness and contentment. Finland lives by 'Sisu' stoic determination, tenacity of purpose, grit, bravery, resilience and hardiness (that explains the ice water swimming).

It is not a coincidence that so many of these concepts originate within the happiest countries in the world. Being from the North of England, I can safely say that enjoying the small things, staying home and being cosy, generally occur thanks to austerity, not happiness – and that is exactly what I mean about mindset playing a big part in happiness.

Mindset and gratitude are closely aligned. Throughout history and around the world, religious leaders and philosophers have commended the virtue of gratitude. Gratitude means different things to different people in different contexts, but it is almost a glue that holds society together – seeing the positive and understanding what has influenced that positive.

Although practicing gratitude has been popular of late, it is not simply a cultural construct developed by retailers. Gratitude has deep roots in human evolution. Animals engage in activities that help another member of their species, knowing that they may return the favour in the future. Studies have found that chimpanzees are more likely to share food with a chimpanzee that had groomed them earlier in the day and are more likely to help another chimpanzee if that chimpanzee had previously helped them.

The Danes do it again – 'Arbedjsglæde' is a common word in Denmark, which means happiness at work. The happiness that we derive from 'doing' something. An emotion and sense of wellbeing that comes when we feel good about the work we do and when we feel involved in the purpose. The UK workplaces, on the other hand, well, they do not help matters much. BITC[62] found that in the UK alone, two in five employees have reported experiencing poor mental health symptoms related to work in the last year; 24% cited bullying and harassment from their manager as a cause; 62% of managers admit that they have had to put the interests of their organization above staff wellbeing; and 33% of those who experienced mental health challenges because of work cited organizational change being handled poorly.

When considering a typical career in the United Kingdom, this means working a whooping 95,000 hours and taking 8,000 hours annual leave. To be happy, we need workplace cultures that enable people to thrive as humans. Unfortunately, all too often, this is just not the case.

How often do you, team members or friends consider quitting your jobs? It may be that you feel you are not being paid enough for the effort and contribution you make, the colleagues who take your ideas, gossip, and create divides, dinosaur-esque management styles or too much pressure and not enough work/life balance.

Leaders, please note that making anybody feel like sh*t for your own pleasure, insecurities, lack of emotional intelligence or to feed power trips, or any other behaviours that dehumanize do not belong in the workplace; they do not belong anywhere. Those behaviours make people unhappy. Period.

This is not me being 'fluffy.' Put your people first, enable happiness through a workplace where people can thrive, and your business will only benefit. Achor[63] found that a company with happy employees could increase their sales by 37% and productivity by 31%, which directly contributes toward building a high-performance work environment and improves the quality of life for all people involved with the work. Then we should consider the impact of happiness on staff turnover, sickness and absence, human errors and your customers!

When somebody smiles, you smile back, right? Happiness breeds happiness, positivity and resilience. Likewise, I am sure we can think of a mood hoover – that person that you do everything possible to just avoid bumping into.

Workplace happiness is experienced when:

→ We have autonomy and decision-making.
→ We enjoy doing the tasks involved in our roles.
→ We feel good about the people we are working with.

→ We are happy with the financial benefits we get from the job.

→ We have opportunities to learn and grow.

→ We feel supported and respected.

→ We experience healthy challenges.

→ We receive feedback.

→ Our physical surroundings meet our needs.

A human-centric workplace is a happy workplace that consistently evolves, knowing that happiness is not a destination but a direction. Connection, belonging, and purpose are the beating heart of the human-centric workplace, embodied by human leaders who want their people to thrive at work and in life.

## CULTURE INDICATOR #3: PSYCHOLOGICAL SAFETY

Bringing our whole selves to work is about showing up, being authentic, vulnerable and maintaining healthy boundaries; sharing what you choose to share. It is about having trust that you feel safe to have a voice and be heard while showing respect toward the person(s) receiving the information.

It may be through what you wear, tattoos, hair colour, piercings, your diet, whether you decide to run a book club with colleagues after work or whether you work flexible hours to schedule family time or even a hobby. For me it is being unafraid of saying 'wife' instead of 'partner', the ability to reach out to a colleague when having a bad day and the simple things like sharing what I have done at the weekend.

Who we are, the talents we were born with, the skills we have learned, the experiences that have shaped us – all of these aspects not only make us unique, but they make us worthy of having the courage to show up.

We must approach the idea of 'whole self' with caution, as we all have inner challenges and demons that need to be handled with care. We also all have different levels of what we choose to share about ourselves, whether it be due to past experiences, our perceptions of privilege (or lack of) or societal norms.

The concept of bringing your whole self is merely an invitation to be more open and to show more of your personality, your talents, your flaws and your skills. Crucially, it is about having a choice.

I have learned first-hand that bringing your whole self does come with risks. Some have not been able to handle my whole self when it has meant maintaining integrity, saying no or speaking up for what I believe in. I will not be bought with pleasantries when cans are being kicked down the road, and I will not stay quiet when my red lines are being crossed. Sitting back, doing nothing – that is not me bringing my whole self. It is amazingly easy for people to perceive action as troublemaking and silence as acceptance. It is not as simple as this. Sometimes I would speak out there and then, sometimes I would zone out, knowing it was not the right time, place or people, and consequently I would take it home with me and toss and turn in bed until I made sense of what I needed to do next.

Creating a human-centric workplace does not need magic ingredients and a swish of a wand; it needs conscious and continued effort to listen and meet the needs and expectations of the people. Adapted from Maslow's Hierarchy of Needs, I offer a basic framework of six key building blocks that will enable your people to bring their whole selves to work, thrive and achieve their potential within the new world of work.

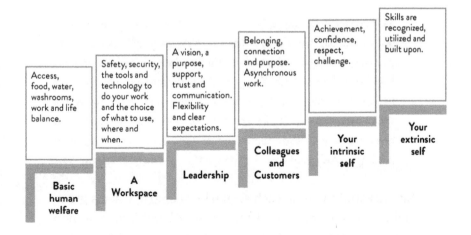

No matter the age, gender, race, religion, sexual orientation or mental health experiences, we all have days when we are not in top form. We may have had a bad night's sleep, a bus may have splashed us on the way to the office, public transport may have been overcrowded and running late, we may have gotten out the wrong side of the bed (apparently, I did that a lot as a teenager) ... there may not be any reason at all.

A human-centric workplace embraces all people and feelings; it consciously knows that this is the way to get the best from your people. When was the last time you were at work and knew you was truly being yourself? Imagine your boss asking how you are – how would you respond?

SCENARIO A: You reply, saying, "Fine thanks, you?" A short conversation follows; you push your feelings down and go in opposite directions to tackle the rest of your day.

SCENARIO B: You reply, saying, "I've had a bad morning" A conversation follows, your boss tells you to "get on with it and don't allow your emotions to affect your work." You are left feeling alone, misunderstood, not heard or feeling cared about. You feel like just a number.

SCENARIO C: You reply, saying, "Thanks for asking, I'm having a bit of a bad day, I'm ready for a coffee. How are you?" Your boss tells you they have also had a bad morning and says they hope the day gets better for you both. You go to the bathroom and when you get to your desk, there's a freshly brewed coffee waiting for you with a sticky note with a smiley face on it. In this scenario, vulnerability has been shared, you have a connection and know that somebody cares. It is highly likely your boss also feels better for doing something nice.

Sit back and imagine each scenario. Scenario C feels great, right? This is not anything ground-breaking, common sense sometimes needs reiterating, but what a difference it can make when you allow yourself to share how you feel and when somebody holds that unconditional positive regard and just does something nice.

How would you respond to your team member? For scenario C to happen, it takes a certain organizational culture – one of transparency, emotional intelligence, honesty, trust, vulnerability, some of the things that make us human.

This human-centric workplace is far from being a given and needs more focus and effort to achieve and evolve. Calling all leaders, this is about integrity, values and quite simply, not being a d*ck. The cost of not doing better can only be compared to that of an earthquake: there are tremors, the epicentre of the event and the far-reaching impacts.

In a world of technology and automation, it is not more robots we need, it is more human behaviour: empathy, trust, compassion, listening, authenticity and connection.

For an individual to have psychological safety is to have the deep-down belief that they can make mistakes without being punished, they have the comfort to show up, to be seen and heard

To have psychological safety should not be a big ask. Nobody is perfect; making mistakes is part of human nature, it is how we learn, build resilience, build connections and innovate. As I have grown older, gained more experiences and listened to people share their experiences, the one thing that has become apparent to me is that we are all 'winging it' at some point, whether it be at work, in parenthood or general life. And yet, so many of us hold back due to the fear of making mistakes – unconditional positive regard is crucial for all humans.

> "When perfectionism is driving, shame is riding shotgun, and fear is that annoying backseat driver."[64]

For you and your team to thrive, people must feel comfortable sharing their thoughts, concerns, questions, ideas and mistakes, all without fear. Without the fear of being shamed, disregarded or criticized. Such psychological safety breeds calculated risk taking, and the speaking of minds and creativity, all of which paves the way for innovations that could be the difference between people and the organization thriving or expiring.

> "... For an organization to truly thrive in a world where innovation can make the difference between success and failure, it is not enough to hire smart, motivated people. Knowledgeable, skilled, well-meaning people cannot always contribute what they know ..."[65]

Abraham Maslow highlighted that in any given moment, as humans, we have two options: step forward into growth or step back into safety. Where teams have psychologically safety, stepping forward is equally as safe as stepping backward.

Google[66] carried out research to answer the question: "What makes a team effective at Google?" They found what mattered most was not who was on the team, but how the team worked together. Psychological safety was deemed the most important – the ability to take risks and feel confident that no one will embarrass or punish anyone else for admitting a mistake, asking a question or offering a new idea. Followed by dependability, structure, and clarity, meaning and impact.

> "The Google researchers found that individuals on teams with higher psychological safety are less likely to leave Google, they're more likely to harness the power of diverse ideas from their teammates, they bring in more revenue, and they're rated as effective twice as often by executives."

When I was starting out in my career, I had a manager who celebrated the fact that I would say, "I don't know, I'll find out." Fifteen years on, I still regularly speak to them and they still refer to that same basic principle. For years they have given me all the credit, without realizing that the reason I responded like that was because they created the environment for me to be honest and vulnerable, without judgment. This is because as a manager, they did not bury their head in the sand, shying away from issues, they ran at them head on to resolve them and make the workplace a better place for everybody.

In a later role, I experienced situations where not having the answers was a sign of weakness, almost incompetence. In those environments, I stopped saying I did not know and instead became the person I did not want to be, somebody who blagged. Berating your team is not recommended, and neither is faking it to your boss. The worst bit was I knew I was blagging, they knew I was blagging, and yet because there was no psychological safety, I could not bring myself to own up to it. Ultimately, we did not have the right answers. I felt like a fraud and they felt frustrated – nobody won.

On a regular basis, whatever my boss did (or did not do) resulted in my chimp taking over my brain. My brain processed the events as a life-or-death situation, the amygdala went into fight or flight, I lost the ability to reason, became anxious and stressed and imposter phenomenon raised its ugly head. This was not a one-off situation and, as such, the more it happened, the more my brain expected it to happen, and the quicker it happened. The whole situation was quite stressful. Now I am not saying stress is bad; some stress keeps us on our toes, but there needs to be a balance and, after a few years, the balance was out of kilter.

Japan, to-date, are the only country who have a word for death from overworking: Karoshi (過労死), with the most common causes being heart attacks and strokes due to stress and a starvation diet, something which has been a challenge for the country dating back to the 90s.

A study by the World Health Organization and the International Labour Organization[67] found that 745,000 people died in 2016 from stroke and ischemic heart disease as a direct result of having worked at least 55 hours a week, a 29 per cent increase since 2000. For the first time on a global scale, long hours at work have been established as responsible for about one-third of all deaths.

Despite all the awareness and warnings, things are only getting worse, during the pandemic research has highlighted that the average working day has extended by 48 minutes.[68]

The optimum spot where the brain functions best in terms of arousal is termed the 'window of tolerance.'[69] The window of tolerance determines how critical or creative we are, how we learn and process and how we relate to ourselves and how we connect to those around us. When we feel safe, when we are in our window of tolerance, we become more open-minded, resilient, creative and motivated.

I have adapted the 'Window of Tolerance' model and applied it to the impact of leadership on an individual within the workplace.

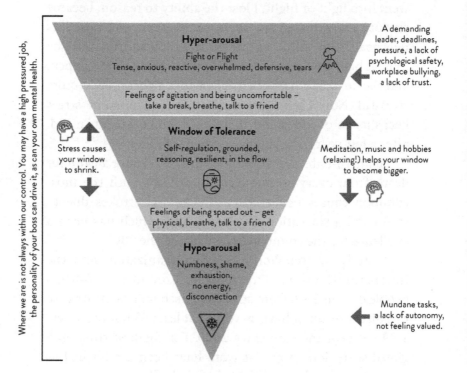

Leaders who demand too much too often from their team, do not trust, or drive a culture of perfectionism will directly impact the window of tolerance of the team around them and push them into hyper-arousal – brains are in stress mode and looking for danger.

When a team member is bored due to mundane tasks, when they lack autonomy or do not feel valued, they will check out, mentally, lacking in motivation and energy – hypo-arousal.

To sustain team members within the window of toler-ance, firstly, the bigger it is the better. The bigger it is the more our brain will function well, the more we will reflect, think rationally and handle emotions.

Leaders, this starts with ensuring that your team members have downtime to relax and recharge (yes, stop contacting them when they are on annual leave). Recognize the feelings of your team member, accept and allow it, investigate the cause and nurture by providing what they need. Coach your team member to be self-aware and know when they are heading into hyper-/hypo-arousal.

Individuals, practice mindfulness and breathing to help remain grounded. When feeling aroused, get physical, burn the energy if in hyper-arousal, light exercise if in hypo-arousal. Get writing – a journal will help to process thoughts and feelings. Talk to somebody. Anybody.

Leaders showing vulnerability, talking about their mistakes, worries and feelings, underpins a culture of psychological safety. The role modelling allows those around them to replicate, knowing that they will not be shamed, disregarded or criticized but listened to, heard, supported and challenged (healthy challenge, that is).

I reflect on one situation where I received a phone call to attend my workplace due to an issue in the swimming pool plant room. Ten-plus emergency vehicles, lots of paperwork, and many hours later, we discovered that somebody working earlier in the day had filled up the chemical tanks with the wrong chemical and inadvertently formed chlorine gas. Yes, it was stressful.

However, the emergency services gave us a glowing report for our emergency operating procedures and my team member apologized like I have never heard anybody apologize. And yet, they still feared that they had lost their job.

Instead of taking a knee-jerk decision, I stepped back, asked lots of questions, reflected on what I could have done differently as a manager, reviewed procedures and delivered refresher training. I learned a lot that day about my team, myself and the way I lead. My team member was forever grateful for the support (and the forgiveness they thought was required), we both learned together, and moved on together.

Psychological safety, knowing that mistakes happen, and that it is okay, leads to increased confidence, creativity, trust, and productivity and helps maintain the window of tolerance. We need team members to question, be curious, assess risks and be open to discussing what is and is not working. To measure psychological safety, take a moment to reflect on:

→ Are mistakes held against you?
→ Can you have a tough conversation with your manager?
→ Do you feel like you are treated equally?
→ Do you feel safe taking risks?
→ Do you find it difficult asking your manager for help?
→ Do you feel like your skills and efforts are recognized and valid?

Amy Edmonson[70] highlights three key things individuals can do to increase a team's psychological safety: frame the work as a learning problem, not an execution problem, acknowledge your own fallibility and model curiosity and ask lots of questions.

In one-to-one situations, a leader should ensure they are approachable for conversations, remain engaged in them and avoid interrupting, show understanding via body language, express gratitude for contributions, build rapport and relationships – get to know your team member, be vulnerable as a leader – talk about your experiences, mistakes and feelings and encourage calculated risk taking and explain your reasoning for doing so.

In group situations, a leader should encourage psychological safety through celebrating ideas and questions and putting a stop to any behaviours that prevent people from speaking up. Invite questions, encourage measurement of what is and is not working and celebrate efforts, not just results.

On an individual front, increase your own psychological safety by empowering yourself to feel psychologically safe through embracing the mindset and forming your internal dialogue. Allow yourself to be vulnerable, to accept that you make mistakes, offer the benefit of doubt to those around you – safety breeds safety.

Remember, you also have the choice of finding a new job. That may sound a little too much, however, so many people accept poor cultures, avoiding putting their heads above the parapet to stay on the side of senior managers and avoid being labelled as causing trouble ... just to keep the job that they dislike and/or are not thriving in anyway. Financial security has a lot to blame for this. When there is financial security, people are more inclined to take risks, to speak out, to make mistakes.

A human-centric workplace embraces mistakes; mistakes can be recovered from, they allow us to grow. Do not panic, remember GOATS.

→ G – Ground yourself – take a breath and talk to somebody before you claim that you best start looking for a new job.
→ O – Own it – We all make mistakes, just do not let somebody else report on yours; it will look like you are trying to hide it and that breach in trust will likely cause more damage than the mistake itself.
→ A – Action – it could be an apology, an IOU, or some actions to resolve.

→ T – Time – Reflect, why was the mistake made?
Is there something bigger happening? You may be
overworked, under pressure, tired ... be kind to
yourself and remember, you are human.

→ S – Show – Demonstrate how you are taking steps to
ensure it is not repeated.

It takes courage to speak out and to take risks, and even
more so in an environment lacking in psychological safety
but doing so is the only option if you want to bring your
whole self to work and live authentically.

"Vulnerability sounds like truth and feels like courage. Truth and
courage aren't always comfortable, but they're never weaknesses."[71]

## CULTURE INDICATOR #4:
## RECRUITMENT AND RETENTION

As we have seen with the battle of the caterpillars – Marks and
Spencer's Colin and Lidl's Cuthbert – almost any idea can be
duplicated. Patents, trademarks and secret ingredients do not
mean diddly squat if your competitor takes the core of what
you do and takes it to the next level, rendering you obsolete.

Your organization's culture is the only real competitive
advantage you have.

Does your organization have people fighting for a role
with you or are you reposting the same advert, multiple
times with different job titles and salaries to lure somebody
into the lion's den?

We have all had those experiences when you visit a new
bar or restaurant, look around, pick up on the vibes and
quickly vacate while avoiding eye contact with anybody
who works there. You are then very quick to tell as many

people as possible what an awful place you thought it was – and thanks to social media, there is no holding back.

The same happens with workplaces. If it is a bad experience, you look to leave and give your opinions to your friends and the internet along the way. In a human-centric workplace, team members not only enjoy working for the organization because they are thriving, but they are your best recruiters because they grab their friends and tell them they must come and experience the joys too.

When recruiting, an organization with the people at the heart protects and defends the culture to the tenth degree; culture fit is not sacrificed for any amount of skill, talent and experience. Skills can be taught, attitudes cannot. Being human, and human-centric, comes naturally to some more than others – but even King Louie, an orangutan from one of my favourite childhood films, said he can learn to be human, so I like to think there is hope for anybody!

Maintaining culture during recruitment is not just about hiring people who, metaphorically speaking, will walk and talk like us. Cultures need fresh blood, diversity and new ways of thinking, not cookie cutters. This makes culture fit not just important, but culture add, crucial.

A human-centric workplace will still lose people along the way, but it is the way and why they lose people that differs. There are many positives as to why people change jobs: a new challenge, progression, change, relocation or a change of career, and when those people leave the door is left open for them. The latest figures show that people are likely to remain in their current roles for two to five years, and this changes across generations.

Team members moving on can be positive, for both themselves and the business, under the right circumstances. For an individual, when values, behaviours and vision are not aligned to the organization, it is perfectly fine, brilliant in fact, to want more, to not have been institutionalized or compromised by a culture that is not in keeping with their core values. People want to work for an organization where they feel aligned.

The parallel scenario is when people realize that enough is enough, and far too often, people leave an organization for negative reasons. Such expensive mistakes include:

→ Misaligned vision and leadership.
→ Compromised values and beliefs causing increased toxicity.
→ A lack of connection, appreciation, belonging and empathy.
→ A lack of trust and autonomy.
→ Uncertainty during hard times and massive change.
→ Organizational structures and processes that create stagnation and frustration.
→ Poor management.
→ A lack of opportunities / a poor customer base.

Walking away is quite often perceived as giving in or giving up, like it is a negative thing. However, if you truly feel like you have given your all, and you are at the point where your values, wellbeing and self-worth are taking a knock, the best thing for you is to let go. Despite the words we may use, this is not about giving in or giving up. The words we use matter.

Telling yourself that you give in is telling yourself that you submit, you are tapping out. It feels as if you are selling yourself short, that the struggle and fear have made you crumble to give way to something else.

Telling yourself that you give up is telling yourself that you are not good enough, you have failed, lost all belief and are going to stop trying. This thought pattern is rooted in regret; you will always be wondering what could have been.

Another phrase often used is, "It is what it is." This just amplifies the frustration. A part of you just screams back, "But wwwhhhhhhyyyy!" But it is a situation that cannot be changed and just must be accepted.

If you want to free yourself from something that no longer serves a purpose to you, we must let go. Letting go is liberating, releasing something that does not work anymore, choosing your battles and looking after your own needs.

Letting go is hard, so we often repress to forget and, in the process, we devalue our own emotions. But clearly, letting go is the utopia – it allows us to move forward before negative emotions manifest in ways we do not expect such as projecting anger onto others, emotional instability, dissatisfaction, stress and disconnection. When we observe, rather than react, we take our power back. For an individual, when is enough, enough?

Ask yourself a few key questions:

→ How does the situation fit with my values?
→ What matters most?
→ Why am I doing it?
→ Who am I doing it for?
→ Am I willing to fight for it?
→ Am I willing to sacrifice for it?
→ Am I willing to pay for it?
→ Am I willing to spend time on it?

A human-centric workplace embraces choice and change, welcomes the right people with open arms and leaves the door open for their future return.

A last-ditch attempt at keeping an employee away from the exit door often involves the offering of more money, but as highlighted in an earlier chapter, money will only motivate for one to three wage slips and, in this instance, it leaves the person wondering why it took a resignation to be offered a raise.

I can see why organizations try the last-ditch attempt. Sometimes they genuinely do not want to lose a valued member of the team, and other times, they fear change and want to avoid the hassle. Another reason could be the cost implications. Oxford Economics[72] revealed that replacing a member of staff incurs significant costs –£30,614 per employee – in lost output and the logistical cost of recruiting.

Offering wage increases to tempt an employee away from moving on is putting a plaster on a gangrene wound. Rip the plaster off and get to the source of the infection before it spreads.

Capture turnover rates in a meaningful way; the data needs to be seen in context, and again, triangulated where possible.

## CULTURE INDICATOR #5: CUSTOMER SATISFACTION

Business is built upon customer relationships and, with the culture of an organization reverberating across all aspects of the business, it represents the way you do business. Measuring customer satisfaction via Net Promoter Score, surveys, the number of complaints, the satisfaction of the complaint resolution and market share is crucial. It is your identity, your image, and it will determine how your people and customers perceive the organization.

Customer satisfaction has varying components: experience and interactions, complaint handling, the ethos, emotional connection such as trust, and ethics such as reputation, transparency and integrity. Any organization that consistently disappoints its customers is unlikely to receive repeat business and, unless it is a monopoly, will almost certainly start to lose market share.

With so much market competition, so much adoption of social media, there is nowhere to hide and being anything but 'human' with your team members is not an option if you want to retain your existing customer base and grow.

The Institute of Customer Service (ICS) has established a clear connection between customer satisfaction and financial performance. Its 2021 index shows, for example, banks whose customer satisfaction was at least one point better than the sector average recorded an average of 2,677 net current account gains, compared to 1,794 net losses for those with a UKCSI score at least one point below the sector average.[73]

A human-centric workplace creates a positive environment for team members with trust, respect, communication and responsibility at the core. Engaged team members who thrive want the opportunity to shine, to achieve, to take ownership – this has a direct impact on the experience your customers receive, as does the impact of having team members who genuinely care – they want to represent the company in the best possible light.

Customers know when they are speaking to somebody who is enthusiastic, positive and genuinely trying to help compared with somebody who is clock watching. Happy people, happy customers. Your people are building the impression and reputation of the company. People buy from people. Team members need to connect with the customer, understand their needs and find solutions to meet them.

Just 11% of customers would repurchase from an organization following a bad experience with an employee, while 43% of customers would also actively warn others against using the organization. For every one-point increase in employee engagement, customer satisfaction rises by 0.41 points.[74] A human-centric workplace looks after their people, knowing that in turn they will look after customers.

# CULTURE INDICATOR #6:
# SUSTAINABILITY,
# IMPACT AND THE CLIMATE

With the rise of awareness about the impact human life has had and continues to have on our planet, team members want more than just a job – they want to work for an organization that gives something back to society. A human-centric workplace incorporates a robust corporate social responsibility culture, one that benefits individual employees, the local community and the planet.

We see communities – whole countries, even – in crisis, and the thing that always stands out is that there is always another person wanting to help people; it is our human instinct to look after our tribes. But collectively we can do more.

In 2021, an estimated 235 million people were deemed in need of humanitarian assistance; that is 1 in 33 people. The international humanitarian assistance from governments and private donors continued to increase, reaching US$35 billion, representing a growth of more than a third since 2014. The UN and partner organizations are targeting to assist 160 million of the 235 million people across 56 countries.[75] Yes, your maths is correct, that leaves 75 million people in need of aid who are not being reached.

There is an estimated eight billion people in the world with US$80 trillion in circulation, with just eight men owning the same wealth as the poorest half of the world (OXFAM 2017). A FTSE-100 CEO earns as much in a year as 10,000 people working in garment factories in Bangladesh. In the US, new research by economist Thomas Piketty shows that over the last 30 years the growth in the incomes of the bottom 50% has been zero, whereas incomes of the top 1% have grown 300%.[76]

"A world where 1% of humanity controls as much wealth as the bottom 99% will never be stable."[77]

It is reasonable to say that not only can we do more, but we must do more. It does not have to be this way; corporations and the super-rich have the power to change this inequality.

In 2016, the world's 10 biggest corporations together had a revenue greater than that of the government revenue of 180 countries combined.[78] Developing countries lose $100bn every year to tax dodging by corporations[79] and Kenya loses $1.1 billion every year in tax exemptions for corporations – twice its budget for health in a country where women have a 1 in 40 chance of dying in childbirth.[80]

We can create a fairer world based on a more human economy – one in which people, not profit, are the bottom line. OXFAM highlighted that in a human economy:

→ Governments work for the 99% of people, not the 1%.
→ Governments will cooperate, ensuring corporations and rich people pay fair taxes, the environment is protected and workers are paid well.
→ Companies work for the benefit of everyone.
→ Extreme wealth is diluted to end extreme poverty.
→ There is gender equality.
→ Technology is used to transform lives.
→ Renewable energy is at the forefront.
→ We value and measure what really matters – not GDP, but human progress.

More and more people are living in fear. The global military expenditure saw its largest annual increase in a decade, reaching $1917 billion in 2019.[81] We are fighting against ourselves – humanity. There is growing inequality globally, which is pulling societies apart, increasing levels of crime and insecurity, and contributing to the levels of global poverty.

A human-centric workplace is one that gives back to society and the planet, aiming to ensure that more and more people are living in hope.

From paying taxes to employee volunteer days, charitable donations and philanthropy toward community initiatives and, on a macro level, reducing the amount of commuting and food waste and general consumption through business activity, "Local communities – including local business networks – play a prominent role in meeting humanitarian needs."[82]

In the UK and the US, the transport sector is responsible for emitting more greenhouse gases than any other and globally, transport accounts for around a quarter of $CO_2$ emissions, with three quarters of the emissions being road vehicles.[83]

> "... the coronavirus crisis could trigger the largest-ever annual fall in $CO_2$ emissions in 2020, more than during any previous economic crisis or period of war."[84]

Research[85] suggests that reducing your commute by just one day per week could save 379.2kg of $CO_2$ emissions. This amount of carbon is equivalent to 2,433km on a short-haul flight or a passenger trip from London to Istanbul; yet business travel continued to grow globally at a rate of 3–5% each year leading up to the 2020-2021 coronavirus pandemic.

The latest United Nations[86] climate action report calls for a green coronavirus economic recovery to fight global warming. As a result of reduced travel, lower industrial activity and lower electricity generation this year due to the pandemic, emissions are predicted to fall up to 7% in 2020. However, this dip only translates to a 0.01°C reduction of global warming by 2050. A green pandemic recovery, however, can cut up to 25% of the emissions we would expect to see in 2030 based on policies in place before COVID-19.

The human-centric workplace has the potential to drive big and much-needed positive change for our planet.

## CULTURE INDICATOR #7: FINANCES

This one is simple and follows on from culture indicator #6. Human-centric workplaces put people before profit. Now, this is not saying that organizations cannot and should not make a profit, quite the contrary. It is how the organisation makes profit and what the organization chooses to do with such profits that defines the culture of the organization.

Yes, organizations pay dividends, invest into new markets, research and development, marketing, infrastructure, property, team growth and will build cash reserves to secure the organization's future.

But, if the senior leadership team are earning 20 times the amount of the lowest paid worker, and the workplace is in squaller, technology is outdated, only basic benefits are in place, there is minimal training provision, cheap toilet roll and awful instant coffee – this is not a human-centric workplace.

A human-centric workplace values each and everybody's contribution, paying fairly in line with contribution, experience, skills and market rate. The progression and continued development of the people is invested in, as is their health and futures through healthcare schemes and pension contributions. The organization has a social conscience, considering wider societal impact and wants to create a better world. Human-centric workplaces ensure the hygiene factors are a given and then offer additional benefits across health, financial and life.

**HYGIENE FACTORS**
- Salary
- Sufficient staffing and resourcing
- Holiday allowances
- Overtime/flextime
- Flexible working
- The physical environment
- Tools, technology and systems
- On-site showering facilities
- Good coffee
- Healthy snacks
- Paid sick leave
- Family friendly policies
  (parental leave, bereavement leave, childcare benefits)
- Appreciation programs
- Employee development plans
- Social Events
- Expenses reimbursed

**HEALTH**
- Discounted gym memberships
- Mental health days
- Healthcare cash plan
- Employee asssitance programs
- On-site exercise provision

**FINANCIALS**
- Shares
- Income protection
- Critical illness cover
- Medical insurance
- Product/service discounts
- Supplemented canteen provision
- Peformance bonus
- Charitable donations at source

**LIFE**
- Volunteering time
- Sabaticals
- Childcare provision
- Homeworking equipment provision
- Above statutory maternity leave
- Legal assistance
- Travel Insurance
- CSR initiatives
- Investments into renewable energy sources

# CULTURE INDICATOR #8:
# INNOVATION

Technology has and continues to change the way we live, consume, socialize and work. With the Fourth Industrial Revolution comes the blurring of boundaries between the physical and digital worlds – advances in artificial intelligence, robotics, the Internet of Things (IoT), 3D printing, blockchain, virtual reality, genetic engineering, quantum computing and other technologies such as the use of renewable energy. Such innovations are the force behind many aspects of modern life, from apps such as Waze and What-3Words, virtual assistants such as Alexa, targeted Netflix recommendations and Facebook's ability to recognize a face and tag it in a friend's photograph.

Some sectors are experiencing fast and disruptive changes, while others are evolving at a slower pace. Success in the Fourth Industrial Revolution naturally requires that our industries use the best available technologies. But technologies alone are not the answer; they need coupling with human factors such as empathy, compassion, agility, change and adaptation.

> "The changes are so profound that, from the perspective of human history, there has never been a time of greater promise or potential peril."[87]

Does the way sh\*t get done ever change? Is the mere suggestion of a new idea quashed? Or do leaders cultivate an environment that nurtures and embraces revolutionary thinking? A culture of innovation is not an accident, but when team members have wings to fly, they must also feel comfort in the roots that ground and secure them.

As we experience more and more technology and innovations within our home lives, the advances are transforming customer expectations and, now more than ever, customers are happy to switch suppliers and brands for a better experience. If we take the concept of the Time, Quality and Cost triangle,[88] having just two of these aspects is now not enough; our customers increasingly expect all three.

A human-centric workplace fosters innovation, not savoured for the sphere of top leadership but innovations that come from anyone in the organization; or in fact externally. It requires: Diversity + Talent + Knowledge + Psychological Safety + Trust + Autonomy + Leadership Support.

I know from writing this book that setting time aside to almost force your brain to be creative, to innovate, is not necessarily always the best way to get your brain going, and yet, without the time set aside, there is no way it would get done; life would take over. Team members must be given the capacity to think, to step back, to get on top of the challenge and have the freedom to fail, rather than be in the challenge and swimming rapidly to stay afloat.

It is not just a lack of innovation that causes issues for organizations, but too much innovation is equally as damaging, with people suffering from innovation fatigue and feeling overwhelmed and pressured. In addition to this is the problem I hear many times, that the idea was too soon for its time – the world was not ready for it.

A human-centric workplace listens to all ideas but validates them and capitalizes on those that fit core competencies, taking a design-thinking approach, testing before scaling and investing in those ideas that are scalable.

# CULTURE INDICATOR #9: PRODUCTIVITY

Watching the Oxford Cambridge boat race got me thinking about productivity, performance and teamwork, and the way in which they all link, rely on and feed each other. A group of people are solely responsible for the speed, balance, rhythm and run of the boat; a performance where one small movement severely affects the outcome, a team fights to stay in sync by just feeling the flow of the bodies around them.

Whether it be hybrid working, space booking, visitor management or workplace design such as the use of colour, biophilia, layouts, acoustics and lighting, everywhere I turn somebody is promising to improve workplace productivity. Not many of the claims are based on actual science. Not many of the claims are measured. Not many of the claims even understand how their tools can improve productivity. But it sounds great.

'Performance' and 'productivity' are often confused within the workplace. In the same way that performance management is about making sure an individual is meeting organizational goals in an effective way, a high-performing team is one that is highly focused on the goals and achieves beyond them.

Performance = The act of doing something and how well it is being done (the effort, the quality).

Productivity = Volume of Input, Volume of Output (the end result, the quantity).

During the 2020/2021 coronavirus pandemic, it has been reported that remote working productivity has increased for some and decreased for others. In some cases, the volume of input has no doubt decreased thanks to things such as home schooling, but I am yet to see anything that has named performance as a consequence, instead of simply the end goal of productivity. In fact, for many, volume of input has increased, with many reporting working longer hours and struggling to switch off.

There are linear trends between performance and productivity; however, it is not a given. Here plays the part that if we work too many hours, we become less productive and burn out. High performance and good work should be mutually supportive, not bargained in a trade-off. So, why is it that we continue to focus on productivity?

> "Productivity isn't everything, but in the long run it is almost everything. A country's ability to improve its standard of living over time depends almost entirely on its ability to raise its output per worker."[89]

A human-centric workplace focuses on performance, not productivity. If we measure people on input (hours) versus output (what the output was) how do we take into consideration the idle time – people chatting at the water cooler (apparently, we all missed those moments during the global COVID working from home experiment), the wasted time – people working on things that are not adding value – presenteeism – and people p*ssing around because they hate their job.

Productivity is for machines; things are just simpler. Performance is for the human-centric workplace; things are just more complex. A performing team would have the traits of having a shared purpose, effective communication, trust, respect, human leadership, continued learning and psychological safety to speak out, to challenge, to make mistakes.

Your people need to know why they are doing it and who they are doing it for.

On an individual level, a team is only as strong as its weakest link. How do we make sure we are not the weakest link ... and how do we perform so those around us perform better?

→ Track how you are spending your time.
→ Wellbeing: take breaks, exercise, nutrition, sleep, stay hydrated.
→ Set yourself goals and deadlines.
→ Use the two-minute rule: if it can be done within two minutes, do it immediately.
→ Do not get drawn into time-sucking meetings.
→ Do not confuse your brain by trying to multitask.
→ Accept that you will have bad days; no beating yourself up.
→ Avoid the email inbox rabbit hole.
→ Prepare your space; is it somewhere you want to spend time?

There is a sign near the entrance to Cambridge University Boat Club's boat bays, saying in large light blue letters: "This is where we prepare to win races." Having such clarity and a clear purpose of why everybody is in the shared space is key – something that organizations must crack when thinking about what the office is for.

Communication, continuous feedback loops, the right tools, training driven by shared objectives, people working independently and the team performance being regularly reviewed – this is where the magic happens! Human-centric workplaces ensure that every hour is used for the best thing, in the best way. Let us work smarter, not harder.

## CULTURE CHANGE

The world in which we operate is increasingly complex with globalized markets, technological growth exponential and four generations within the workplace. Organizations are required to make changes on a regular basis at a fast pace.

Every culture is unique, it is the DNA of the organization; however, it is also something that will adapt, change and evolve. Triggers may include business strategy, expectations of people, new leadership, the evolution of technology, over or under performance, innovations and/or financial markets, and we should now also include global pandemics.

There are business leaders who, pre-pandemic, were against any form of remote working and expected their teams to be in the office, at a desk, 9–5pm, and by 9–5 they actually meant 8.30–6pm. And now their hand has been forced, they know they have no option but to offer increased flexibility.

On an individual level, we know change is difficult, when we multiply that throughout the organization, the resistance to change is amplified. In fact, reactions to organizational change can be so excessive and immediate that some researchers have suggested it may be easier to start a completely new organization than to try to change an existing one.[90] Okay, so that may sound a little drastic; however, on reflection and thinking about a few companies that spring to my mind, I totally understand that point of view, however impractical and romanticized it is. Genuine culture change, turning the tanker, is not a quick or easy task.

Psychological needs and emotions are heightened during workplace changes due to perceptions of job security, autonomy of voice and fairness that are linked to organizational decisions.

Humans are creatures of habit, and where there is a habit, the information is processed within our unconscious brain;

it is hardwired. As such, the human brain does not like uncertainty, it triggers the danger response. The brain does not know if there is a sabretooth tiger around the corner, so we go into tunnel vision mode to deal with the immediate threat. This action is counterintuitive to rational thinking, which does not exactly help with the dealing of uncertainty.

Research has shown that the brain prefers guaranteed pain over uncertainty, because pain is certain[91] – the study told some people they had a 50% chance of receiving an electric shock and some that they would definitely receive a shock and guess what, it was the 50% facing uncertainty who had higher stress levels. This links back to the brain wanting to conserve energy through automatic, unconscious responses as it scans the environment to determine what is safe and what is not.

Avoiding uncertainty cripples organizations. Instead of making a change and innovating, organizations are often happy to risk the safe route to avoid uncertainty. The thing is, there is no getting away from it; life is uncertain. Resisting uncertainty does not remove it; we live in an increasingly unpredictable world and not everything will go to plan.

To drive culture change, we must drive change to habits. Our people need to be brought along the journey, hearts and minds, and to do so, our leaders are required more than ever to understand the dynamics of human behaviour in the workplace to navigate and manage change journeys.

"The biggest factor in why organizational change fails, involves a failure to change human habits."[92]

When at work, the environment and stimuli result in a certain interaction by each person. When the environment and stimuli are repeated, a habit will form. To change habits, organizations often revert to lots of talking and thinking to raise awareness of the change, which is about to, or has already, happened. But, to profoundly change habits, we must change behaviours in real time.

Genuine culture change, turning the tanker, is not a quick or easy task. It should not start with an executive mandating change, rebranding of the office and the vinyls or simply explaining why change needs to happen. Culture change starts with action. A human-centric workplace gives people a voice and listens. A human-centric workplace does change with the people, not to the people.

## ACTIVITY: WINDOW OF TOLERANCE

Identifying the symptoms you experience to build awareness

Hyper-arousal: How many of these symptoms do you experience at work?

| Anxiety | Impulsivity | Intense Reactions | Lack of Emotional Safety | Hyper-vigilance | Tension | Feeling Overwhelmed |
|---|---|---|---|---|---|---|
| Over-eating | Obsessive thoughts/ behaviours | Tears | Chaotic Responses | Defensiveness | Anger / Rage | Aggression |

The Window of Tolerance: How many of these symptoms do you experience at work?

| Balanced | Calm | Relaxed | A feeling of being in control | Like you can take on any thing the world throws at you | Resilient | Grounded |
|---|---|---|---|---|---|---|

Hypo-arousal: How many of these symptoms do you experience at work?

| No emotions / numbness | Auto-pilot responses | Memory loss | Struggling to process thoughts | Lethargic | Shame | Embarrassment |
|---|---|---|---|---|---|---|
| Depression | Low energy | Cannot say no | Exhaustion | A feeling of being disconnected / lonely | Helplessness | Hopelessness |

What is the severity of your feelings?
For each symptom you experience, rank from 1 to 4, with 1 being least severe and 4 being extreme.

What causes these feelings?

What will you do to regulate yourself?

# KEY TAKEAWAYS

- Culture is the personality of your organization, an ongoing process that belongs to everybody. Culture is not an approach and something you are, it is an outcome of actions, the things you do.
- The human-centric workplace is about integrity, values and quite simply, not being a d*ck.
- Soft skills are not 'soft,' they are critical and underpin the success of your people and the business.
- Making anybody feel like sh*t for your own pleasure, insecurities, lack of emotional intelligence or to feed power trips or any other behaviours that dehumanize, do not belong in the workplace; they do not belong anywhere.
- Our workstyles and behaviours have a wider impact; stop forcing people to commute for an hour to sit in an office every day. Enable change.
- There are eyes and ears everywhere; consciousness and integrity are key.
- We can do better, and we must do better, for the sake of our people, our organizations and our planet.

## REFLECTIONS

- What can you do to drive humanness in your organization?
- How does your organization use the cultural indicators to measure culture?
- How will you regulate yourself and support the people around you to do the same?

# CHAPTER 4

# HUMAN
# LEADERSHIP

A human-centric workplace enables people to thrive through unlocking skill sets and self-belief, trusting, empowering, supporting, challenging and through continuous learning. It is not the job of a leader to make or break somebody. Leaders inspire, influence and impact others in order to improve performance.

'Don't bring me problems, bring me solutions' – this phrase does not belong in any workplace. On one hand, the ill-judged leader, may believe they are empowering people to find solutions, but to the person who cannot find a solution and is seeking support, it leaves them feeling frustrated and demoralized, and it will only be a matter of time that they choose to turn a blind eye to problems they uncover and need wider support to resolve. People making themselves vulnerable and asking for help should be a behaviour that is celebrated, not berated. Leaders are not enabling performance improvement if they are inadvertently encouraging people to wing it, blag it or ignore it.

I am not sure if there is anything more irritating and demotivating than a newly appointed and uninformed manager who swaggers into the office declaring they have an idea of how to change things around here. They arrive, and in an attempt to make their mark, change everything in their path; after all, they are there because you need them. It is this type of behaviour that sets apart managers from leaders.

Power and control are what separate leaders and managers. Managers thrive with circles of power; leaders enable their people to thrive through circles of influence. Anybody can be a leader, but not everybody leads in a way that people follow and not everybody is led in a way that inspires them to lead other people in the same way.

Although experience is important, it is people's skills and talents and how they intend to use those skills and talents, the patterns in the way the leader thinks, feels, behaves, that determine how good of a leader they are.

There is much noise about leaders being born to lead and there are certainly traits that enable somebody to stand out as a leader, such as personality and intelligence, but leadership skills can be learned. Let me repeat: leadership skills can be learned. Anybody can be a leader. Leadership qualities can be identified and acquired and, in this sense, anyone can choose to focus on developing themselves as a human leader. Alongside such leadership qualities, the individual must have a deep understanding of the business and sector alongside the training, support and experience.

There is an abundance of research, theories and models that are based on different ways of thinking. Some focus on traits and qualities, while some touch upon the importance of situational aspects that influence how leaders behave. The greatest tool we have as leaders is ourselves. The ability that we all have – to communicate, to listen, to connect, to empathize, to be creative, to think and to act – to develop human leadership.

Soft skills are not soft; they are almost certainly hard, and we must stop diminishing the power and importance of them. We are all people, people who need security, belonging, love, a challenge, a purpose and to feel compassion and empathy during times of need. Such skills are human skills; they are hard and we all heavily rely on the giving and taking of them.

| A MANAGER | A HUMAN LEADER |
| --- | --- |
| Builds processes | Builds people |
| 'ME' | 'WE' |
| Blames | Fixes |
| Knows | Shows |
| Takes | Gives |
| Commands | Asks |
| Rational is | Visionary is a |
| Stabilizes | Initiates change |
| Power comes with the position | Power comes with the person |
| Does things right | Does the right things |
| Plans | Inspires |
| Organizes | Influences |
| Controls | Trusts |
| Embraces the status quo | Challenges the status quo |
| Documents policy | Trains and teaches |
| Follows rules | Questions the rules |
| Focuses on execution | Focuses on the ideas |
| Risk adverse is | Welcomes risk |
| Impersonal is | Leads with emotional intelligence |
| Focuses on 'how and when?' | Focuses on 'what and why?' |
| Wants efficiency | Wants effectiveness |
| Avoids conflict | Uses conflict to affect change |
| Transacts | Transforms |
| Generates fear | Earns respect |
| Plans the details | Sets the destination |
| Sees problems | Sees opportunities |
| Has an outward focus | Has self-awareness |

Some people will naturally possess advanced skills in some of these areas, whereas others will need to work on them, but they are all workable. We can all be human leaders, we just need to make the choice, set the intention and put the effort in.

> "Leaders are the ones who run headfirst into the unknown, they rush toward the danger, they put their own interests aside to protect us, or to pull us into the future, leaders would sooner sacrifice what is theirs to save what is ours, and would never sacrifice what is ours to save what is theirs. This is what it means to be a leader, it means they choose to go first into danger, headfirst toward the unknown, and when we feel sure they will keep us safe, we will march behind them and work tirelessly to see their visions come to life and proudly call ourselves their followers."[93]

To lead is not easy, but ensuring people are central to the organization should be a given. From gender and pay inequality, wellbeing, trust, productivity, engagement, change management and the impact our working practices are having on the planet, we are getting it all oh-so-very wrong.

Apart from it being the right thing to do, the benefits are clear when leaders adopt a human-centric view of business that emphasizes a culture of respect, trust, compassion and wisdom. Individual wellbeing increases, and the performance of the organization rises as a result of the impacts on the individuals.

Globally, the cost of poor management in 2020 approached $7 trillion – 9% to 10% of the world's GDP.[94]

Most leaders I have worked with and for whom I have tried hard to do everything right on paper, I have not come across many who consciously wanted to cause harm to their employees or the organization. Poor leadership can cause damage to the person, and it almost certainly makes your people less engaged, less loyal, less productive, less well, less committed, less brave, less innovative … and care less; all things that significantly add up to less profit for the organization. The statistics do not lie; the workplace is the source of much pain.

Gallup highlighted, on a global scale, the significant impact that leadership can have on an organization's people. Managers account for at least 70% of the variance in employee engagement scores. Fewer than two in ten employees strongly agree the leadership of their organization communicates effectively with the rest of the organization. Fewer than two in ten employees strongly agree that the leadership of their organization makes them feel enthusiastic about the future. Less than a quarter of employees strongly agree that their performance is managed in a way that motivates them to do outstanding work. Well, those statistics are not exactly inspiring, are they?

When such engagement survey results return, leaders scratch their heads, or worse still, the engagement surveys do not get completed and the dirty laundry is flaunted on sites such as Glassdoor. Either way, it leaves the leader guessing who and why. Glassdoor is an example of an employee desperate to have a voice, a safe place to remain anonymous and avoid any repercussions.

Taylorism is said to be the first management theory; it dates to the 1880s and played a significant role in shaping leadership theories. The core principles were that of carrot-and-stick management. The manager was there to determine the best way for the worker to do their job, and to provide training and incentives for good performance.

Taylorism contributed to many management-thinking techniques, process analysis mapping and optimization, the standardization and documentation of protocol, mass production and efficiency. Taylorism focused achieving maximum efficiency from the workers.

It's 2021 and Taylorism is very much alive and kicking. It was Taylorism that identified that workers need a break; okay, it was that workers needed a break to ensure they are most productive for operations, rather than to promote their wellbeing, but I guess it was a decent start.

Taylorism practiced that it was not enough to assign tasks; supervisors should monitor performance to make certain that workers are implementing the most efficient solutions. Even today I see workplaces where the physical layout was designed so managers can watch their team in order to exert power, pressure and control.

Taylorism did not believe in leaders getting stuck in and getting their hands dirty; role modelling was not part of the theory. Instead, managers planned and trained, and workers executed what they were told to execute.

Today, people do not want to be managed by a boss; they want to follow a leader, to be led by a coach. Traditionally, management was about telling, direction, authority and outcomes. Whereas coaching is about exploring, facilitating, partnerships and long-term improvements, focusing on the development of competent individuals who require guidance but not direction.

To coach a team member is to do whatever it takes to support their best thinking, providing the environment and circumstances to ensure engagement. To coach a team member is to understand and leverage strengths, talents and potential. To coach is to set out and agree on clear expectations. To coach is to know your people through lots of deep conversations and build genuine relationships.

Now, of course, there are circumstances when people need to be managed; for instance, when somebody is new to a situation, lacking in confidence or lacking in ability. To lead effectively, you just need to know when to wear which hat, and that takes experience and a pinch of not-so-common sense.

Gallup also found that one of the most important decisions companies make is simply whom they name manager, yet companies fail to choose the candidate with the right talent and skills for the job 82% of the time. This goes back to talent and skills and is no surprise, really, when only one in 10 people possess the talent and skills to be a leader.[95]

The Peter Principle[96] is a concept that highlighted in 1969 that people within a hierarchy are promoted based on their success in previous jobs and, as such, rise to a level of their incompetence as skills within one role do not translate to another. This concept can be applied to those promoted into leadership roles because they could do their job successfully at an individual level. They find themselves in a role with power and authority, knowledge of the tasks, ways of working and boundaries with the focus of getting the job done. Once the job is done, they receive their reward and repeat the same behaviours to get the next.

Where are we going wrong? The etymology of 'leading' is not about doing, it is about being. Being a certain way to drive forward to the goal. When leading is focusing on doing (i.e. managing/being a boss), work-related trauma is at risk of becoming 'a thing.' *Trauma*, derived from the Greek word meaning 'wound' in its simplest definition is a physical or mental injury. Workplace trauma can derive from:

→ Stressful events (i.e. accident or injury)
→ Organizational stressors (i.e. poor leadership, bullying, threats, harassment, betrayal, chronic pressure, unresolved conflict or toxic work environments)
→ Physical stressors (i.e. noise, chaotic environment, no sense of control over space or fear for physical safety)
→ External threats (i.e. evacuation, lockdown, fire or robbery)

Symptoms of work-related trauma can be physical: aches and pains, changes in appetite, sleep issues, restlessness, panic attacks. Or emotional: irritability, anger, anxiety, cognitive: blaming others, negativity, a lack of focus or memory. Or behavioural: defensiveness, withdrawal, or emotional outbursts.

Whether direct or indirect, sudden or cumulative, organizational trauma is typically fuelled by a lack of communication, trust or control or poorly led organizational change. David Rock[97] says:

> "Although a job is often regarded as a purely economic transaction [...] the brain experiences the workplace first and foremost as a social system. When people feel betrayed or unrecognized [...] they experience it as a neural impulse, as powerful or painful as a blow to the head. Most people who work in companies rationalize or temper their reactions; they 'suck it up,' as the common parlance puts it. But they also limit their commitment and engagement. They become purely transactional employees."

Leaders shape our day-to-day experiences for the good and the bad and that is significantly underestimated. On reflection of leaving a past organization, I said to a close friend that I felt like I had left an abusive relationship. It was a hard thing to say but as time went on I became at peace with it; I unpicked it, I healed, I became more resilient and focused on not just how I could ensure that I was a human-centric leader, but how I could influence others to be so too.

Human-centric leadership is not about perfection; after all, we all have a chimp on our shoulders. Note I said chimp, not chip. Human-centric leadership is about making ourselves vulnerable, putting our best selves forward and being brave enough to inspire. To respect and love equally and be accepting of each contribution. To be conscious of thoughts and actions and to lead with clarity and purpose. To leave baggage behind and embrace with a growth mindset that people learn and change.

Human leaders focus on team togetherness and collaboration, not individual competition and secrecy. Human leaders focus on progress, not perfection. Human leaders focus on the long-term vision and overcome problems and challenges with that in mind; there is no room for short-term fixes. Human leaders are conscious of their own emotions, and others', and lead with consistency. Human leaders are visible and treat people as an individual; copy-and-paste emails are a thing of the past. Human leaders are grateful for the efforts their people put in and the way they follow. Human leaders align their head, heart, gut and actions. Human leaders build relationships and connections; people are never just a cog, never just a number.

The human-centric workplace is fuelled by consciousness. Consciousness to put people over profit, to know right from wrong and make decisions that enable people to thrive, for the good of the organization and wider society, without having a detrimental impact upon our planet.

I am not writing this book to tell you that human-centric leadership is possible, I am writing it to inspire you because it is crucial for us all to handle what the 21$^{st}$ century is throwing at us, within our societies and our planet.

As a leader, you could choose to abuse the power you have been entrusted with, to damage or use the power you have been entrusted with and give it back to your people; to focus on influencing and inspiring to change lives. A human-centric workplace remembers that leadership is an honour.

# SO, WHAT MAKES A
# LEADER WONDERFUL?

A bit like my pantry, there is not one magic sauce (and yes, I am a millennial with a pantry – I am super cool like that). Being a wonderful leader encapsulates many ingredients, just enough of one thing and a bit more of another. Being a wonderful leader is not just about it looking good in the cookbook, it must taste good, too.

Some leaders have left a bad taste in my mouth, and some have left me with an addiction for certain ingredients.

Wonderful leaders know that people are the key to success and encourage them beyond their limiting beliefs. They earn respect and enrich the lives of those who they feel honoured to lead. Wonderful leaders are human leaders, embracing mistakes, supporting during wobbles and practicing vulnerability. Listening more, to understand and to connect and talking less; they do not want to be centre of attention and the best person in the room.

Wonderful leaders are brave and challenging conversations are had without blaming and shaming to encourage growth of the individual, team and organization. Wonderful leaders are authentic and act with integrity; it is these behaviours that build deep trust within their teams. They use their power to fuel their teams, promoting their achievements to drive confidence, self-belief and growth.

Wonderful leaders are conscious of their impact; they build a team environment, encourage the sharing of ideas, information and resources. They are self-aware and know their weaknesses, they ask questions, showing they do not know everything; after all, they are only human. And because they are only human, they themselves will make mistakes.

A Human Leader has integrity and behaves authentically, building loyalty and trust with those around them.

# INTEGRITY AND AUTHENTICITY

There is a story about a graduate being given a book of business wisdom. When opened, the hundreds of pages were blank, except for the first, which says, "Do the right thing."

Integrity is not just one action; it is a state of mind, a way of being. Over the years, I have wasted far too much energy on people who say they have integrity, but do not do the right thing. My one piece of wisdom for you is, please do not waste your energy – put your energy into being different from them and trust that they will be found out in the end.

> "Choosing courage over comfort; choosing what is right over what is fun, fast or easy; and choosing to practice our values rather than simply professing them."[98]

Integrity is an essential component for leadership; where leaders express what they believe (showing honesty) and what they feel (showing authenticity), where they do not hide or misrepresent their thoughts and feelings, where they do not exaggerate or lie, where they follow through on their commitments, walk the talk and practice what they preach, and all of this is consistent. The mindset is that it is better to be honest than to delude people and, in the process, delude yourself. Being economical with the truth will get you nowhere. The leader sets the tone for the team. Without integrity, no success as a leader is conceivable.

The consistency of behaviours builds trust and loyalty. Your people need to know that you will do the right things, for the right reasons, at the right time, regardless of the circumstances. Leaders with integrity are not afraid to face the truth. Integrity means telling the truth, even if the truth is ugly.

Considering the 2020/21 coronavirus pandemic, Gallup[99] conducted research asking followers what they expected from their leaders. With 10,000 interviews held, the data boiled down to four key points. People want their leaders to: tell them the truth, show them they care, keep them safe and give them hope.

According to Freud,[100] we have a pleasure principle (Id) and a reality principle (Ego). The pleasure principle wants to fulfil impulses immediately (have you ever wanted to take a chip of somebody's plate because they looked good?), whereas the reality principle considers the risks and stops us from doing something right there and then that may land us in hot water and instead works to satisfy the urge to make sure the behaviours are safe and appropriate (you buy your own chips!).

The two principles are in a constant battle but being a mature adult is controlling impulses, showing patience, being realistic. The reality principle ensures we see the world as it is and not as we wish it to be in our dreams. As a leader, it stops us from becoming disillusioned. A leader in touch with reality does not hide facts; they are honest and communicates truth in the best way they know how and suitable for the situation. They know that they are responsible for communicating truth, for living and breathing integrity.

A human-centric workplace does not trust luck, hope for miracles, expect rewards without effort, hope that problems go away by themselves or make excuses. The human-centric workplace is not a fantasyland where everything is simply fine and dandy. A human-centric workplace is realistic, accepts challenges and responsibilities, is brave and embraces tough conversations, recognizing individual circumstances and approaching with empathy.

## LOYALTY

In 2012, me and my wife rescued our dog Patsy from a puppy farm. She was underweight, covered in oil and scared. She had never been on a lead and did not know how to play. After six months, she wagged for the first time. Today, she is like a different dog. She is happy, loving and loyal. How did we do it? We took care of all her basic needs, we built trust, we loved her, and we let her recover at her own pace.

Animal experts frequently attribute the loyalty of dogs to a shared history. Canines and humans have evolved together. The link between the two species dates many, many years back (10,000–30,000 years). There are many lessons we should take from dogs.

Dogs are a pack animal; intuition tells them to work together to overcome danger; trusting, cooperating and putting the pack's interests first are all a natural part of surviving. Many people have dog loyalty stories based on their relationship with their dog. Part of this is due to the great communication that exists between dogs and humans. The loyalty of dogs toward their owners also may stem from the fact that dogs view themselves as our equals, not as a separate species.

Dogs are loyal because their basic needs are met, they trust, cooperate, and put their pack first, they love, they have deep connection, they have a way of communicating their needs and they treat us as equals.

Let us look at how loyalty plays out within the workplace. Once people identify you as a leader, loyalty becomes an interesting conundrum. Research tells us that millennials are apparently three times more likely than non-millennials to change jobs and 91% do not expect to stay with their current organizations longer than three years.

However, loyalty has little to do with length of employment or how old people are, but everything to do with actions. Loyal team members work hard for their pay and are committed to company success; they may someday leave, but while they work for you, they do their best and often even put the company's interests ahead of their own.

In a world where remote working is more and more on the rise, loyalty and trust are more important than ever. Inspiring loyalty is a tricky thing; it is intangible. But there are many actions that will certainly help.

Human leadership, to breed loyalty, requires increasing the positive emotions that your employees feel. Understanding that you are dealing with root emotions, rather than the specific behaviours those emotions drive, will keep you focused. Pay must be competitive and fair. Employees expect to be paid as much as they could earn doing the same job someplace else and they feel 'de-valued' when they are paid less.

Loyalty breeds when people are surrounded by those they know, like and trust. An easy way to ensure that connection between employees is to create referral bonuses and have an employee referral program that makes it easier for employees to recommend their friends.

Part of earning an employee's loyalty is showing them that you trust them to do their job. Set goals and give feedback to mould performance positively. Trust feeds loyalty; increase engagement by embracing autonomy. Within the parameters of what is possible, give your people flexibility over hours worked and the location they work from.

Unnecessary uncertainty creates a climate of stress that can make employees miserable. A human-centric workplace focuses on clear, transparent communications and change management.

> "'Change management' is not a downstream plug-in to a workplace project; rather the workplace project is a downstream plug-in to a change journey."[101]

It is difficult for employees to feel loyal to a company that tolerates individuals who make the workplace miserable for everyone else. In a human-centric workplace, nobody is above the law – both written and the unwritten rules.

Employees want to be proud of their jobs and of where they work. Companies that have impressive talent brands attract and retain talent more easily.

If you are throwing employees into situations in which they do not feel comfortable or expecting them to meet goals with broken, outdated or less-than-useful equipment, there will be problems. And those problems, no matter what you might like to think, are your responsibility. Give your team members room to grow, educate and equip them; the benefits are endless.

You do not want issues to fester. Keep your eyes and ears open (and tell your management to do the same). Look for warning signs before things come to a head. And when you spot an issue, deal with it sooner than later, but deal with it fairly. As a leader, the last thing you want is for everyone under you to tag you as a fake. Be authentic, give and expect to receive respect.

You do not have to implement all these practices at once. Start small and work up from there. Loyalty builds cumulatively; employees gradually respond to changes in behaviour, management style and company performance. So, every little bit, every positive action, every improvement, every appropriate response to a challenge adds up. It is important to take stock of where you are at, where you want to be, and how you plan to get there, but it is more important to act. Build on good behaviours and go forward from there.

On one level I would argue that there is no such thing as being 'too loyal,' as I simply cannot see any downsides; loyalty is the glue that binds individuals into teams and teams into an organization. However, as I said, loyal employees often put the organization's needs before their own, and herein lies a problem.

A worker slogging their guts out for an organization comes from a genuine place, a motivation they must just do their best. It is about the values they hold, the pride they feel when doing a good job, the relationships with customers, a purpose, a challenge, to simply achieve.

However, sometimes it does go too far. It goes too far when organizations forget that individuals work both for the company, and themselves, when cultures dehumanize, when expectations far outweigh the rewards and when people cannot have a day off without being contacted.

→ Loyalty is not about allegiances.
→ Loyalty is not about saying what you think your boss needs to hear.
→ Loyalty is not about agreeing with everything your organization does.
→ Loyalty is not about working on your day off.
→ Loyalty is not about working yourself into the ground.
→ Loyalty is not about control.
→ Loyalty is not about spinning the worst behaviours into heroism.
→ Loyalty is not about tolerating.

The real meaning of loyalty is knowing deep down that, through good times and bad, those around you have got your back, because they also know that you have theirs.

→ Loyalty is about having straight and difficult conversations with an individual.

→ Loyalty is about not agreeing but having a debate and feeling safe to do so.

→ Loyalty is about showing how you as a team member fit with the company future.

→ Loyalty is about disagreeing, but in private.

→ Loyalty is about making sure a team member is looking after themselves.

→ Loyalty is about investing, learning and development, and progression and promoting within.

→ Loyalty is about supporting somebody during a difficult time.

→ Loyalty is about rewarding the right behaviours.

→ Loyalty is about fairness and mutual respect.

Bad leaders expect loyalty; it allows them to behave in ways that ultimately create toxic workplace cultures. Good leaders earn loyalty because they inspire principles that mutually benefit everybody. Within the human-centric workplace, leadership fuels mutual loyalty, maintains healthy boundaries and reaps the benefits as a result.

## "TRUST ME," SAID THE MANAGER

Like integrity, trust is a way of being, not a way of doing. Trust is the feeling that somebody or something can be relied upon. You may not have cold hard facts to prove it, but deep down, you are sure that it will turn out to be good,

Inspiring trust and trusting others is essential. As a leader, being trustworthy is the cornerstone to motivating and inspiring and building effective and functional teams.

As a team member, when we enter a relationship with an organization, i.e. from interviewee to employee, we are ultimately signalling to that company that we trust them. We trust the organization that what they said during the interview process regarding the role and the culture of the organization and the rewards and recognition are correct. We trust them to pay us the agreed wage at the agreed time, to enable us to provide for ourselves and our families. We trust them to lead us in line with the culture 'advertised.' We trust them with our development and progression. We trust them to not do anything to damage our wellbeing (physical, emotional or psychological). We trust that they will act with integrity.

The trust built between the leader and team member creates loyalty, a safe place to shelter the storms, increased collaborative thinking and innovation, and is crucial during any workplace change initiatives.

On a neuroscience level, being in an environment lacking in trust manifests into Amygdala Hijack – you become stressed and your brain signals danger. You put walls up and distance yourself from people. You doubt your intuition and it is draining.

The flip side is that oxytocin is released following interactions with those who appear trustworthy. Being trustworthy makes people feel good and when this happens at work, work itself is more likely to be enjoyable.

It is human nature to be a bit wary; it is a good thing, it adds a bit of protection and makes you a bit more cautious. However, if mistrust goes too far, the ability to step outside of the issue and reflect, reason and see the bigger picture narrows, and it becomes a vicious circle from then on.

When trusting, I tend to follow my gut; I will almost certainly trust until I am given a reason to not trust. If your spidey senses are tingling, it may be a past experience, a perception or it could be the other person. For the sake of your own health and relationships, please do not ignore it; try to talk it through with somebody (try a coach or mentor) and see it as an opportunity to grow. Staying in stress mode leads to you feeling on edge and defensive and is generally uncomfortable (for everybody!).

When I hear managers saying, "Trust me," it makes me want to scream. Trust is not about words. Trust is about actions. Trust is a way of being, not a way of doing.

> "Stop asking me to trust you when I'm still coughing up water from the last time you let me drown" (Unknown).

When considering what behaviours make up the way of being that builds trust, leaders require emotional intelligence. Be aware that emotions can drive our behaviour and impact people (positively and negatively) and learn how to manage those emotions – both our own and others. There are five key areas: self-awareness, self-regulation, motivation, empathy, and social skills.[102] Human leaders build trust by:

→ Being honest – Some things are difficult to hear but it is best to hear them (constructively/sensitively) than find them out later and know you have been lied to.
→ Being a role model – Do not do the opposite of what you say you want.
→ Keeping their word – Do what you say and say what you do. If you cannot keep your word, revert to 'be honest.' Be consistent with your performance but also your mood.
→ Being vulnerable – If you do not know something, admit you do not know it. There is not much worse than a boss who is a blagger.

→ Being collaborative – Share information that allows your team to do their job.

→ Listening – Give your team a voice. Listen more than you speak.

→ Through body language – If you avoid eye contact, you will look dodgy and dishonest. If you have your arms folded, you will look defensive. If you look too relaxed, you will look disinterested.

→ Being inclusive – Do things with your people, not to your people.

→ Through getting their hands dirty – Do not sit back and point your finger; now and again, get stuck in. Show your team you believe in the purpose.

→ Being human – Take an interest in their personal lives/hobbies/family and share yours.

I am incredibly lucky to work with people I trust, even when they drag me up 25m high trees, clip me in and kick me off the edge. When my arms and legs went wobbly, I did not hesitate in asking them to help me ... that is trust.

# BOUNCEBACKABILITY

Yes, bouncebackability is an actual word. It entered the Oxford English Dictionary in 2005 thanks to one of my childhood idols, ex-Oldham Athletic football manager, Iain Dowie. Iain coined the phrase to describe how the football team he was managing at the time, Crystal Palace, went from the fringes of relegation in December to winning promotion in May. What Iain Dowie was describing was resilience, the capacity to recover following a setback.

Humans as a species are resilient by nature – how else would we have survived thus far? There is an old Japanese proverb that reads: "Fall seven times, stand up eight." A plain-sailing world with no setbacks, apart from being totally unrealistic, actually sounds quite boring too.

The last year of the global pandemic certainly tested organizations' and people's bouncebackability; collectively we pulled together to find solutions. Quite often technology and empathy were the answers we required.

Workplaces are a source of stress, redundancies, deadlines, organizational change, disaster recovery, competition, politics, technology that does not work, and misaligned values and cultures. The dynamic world we live in requires resilience, now more than ever. We need our people to be tenacious, to welcome challenges, to problem solve and ultimately make the most out of even the worst situations. For this to happen, your people need to know that you, as a leader, have their back.

You may remember the example from an earlier chapter where my boss gave me a dressing down after I presented a piece of work. Instead of apologizing for their behaviour, I later found out that they had told a colleague that I would be fine because I was resilient. Can I just say that, being on the other end of that, at no point did I condone the behaviour and brush it off because I was resilient, so why did it matter that I was treated badly? I replied, "But I should not have to be."

Okay, so younger Simone was optimistically expecting a different type of world, maybe I was a little wet behind the ears. Older Simone, well, older Simone knows that she does have to be resilient, because there is always an ass somewhere out there on a mission to ruin somebody's day. And because I was resilient, the way I handled the situation was fitting; I carried on and proved them wrong. (Ok I am fairly stubborn to which helped!).

Stressors from our home lives also follow us to work; who we are as people does not, and should not, stop at the front door of an office. A human-centric workplace recognizes and embraces team members bringing their whole selves to work and supports them through the difficult times. Whether it be flexibility around working hours, extra time off, paid sick leave, mentoring or coaching, health cash plans ... or just simply asking if they are okay and listening. Human-centric workplaces support their people to build resilience in order to handle the stressors that life throws their way.

Resilient employees are able to manage stress effectively, so it is not overwhelming and detrimental. They practice self-care to avoid burnout, and they are their true authentic self, behaving in line with their core values.[103]

The workplace should not feel like an episode of *Takeshi's Castle*. Nobody needs that many obstacles in day-to-day life; we will become weary, lose our fight and think the world is against us. The need for and use of resilience in a work context needs to be monitored and managed; it needs to be balanced.

On an individual level, building resilience is very much a journey. It takes time, reflection, practice, patience and perspective. Organizations can support that journey through providing the right tools and training in relation to knowledge of how to handle stressful situations, coaching provisions to build confidence and character, having leaders who show they have their team's back and who provide clarity of the purpose of the organization, and the part their team plays. Leaders themselves must also model resilience, it is the only way that resilience will embed into an organization.

Through looking after our emotional and physical health, focusing on the future, and motivating ourselves to get there and through strong and healthy relationships with those around us, we can all be resilient. We should not always have to be, and this is a crucial point. It is okay to not be resilient, it is okay to say you are struggling, it is okay to think that a situation is just a bit too much. Be kind to yourself, look after yourself and connect with those around you for some support.

Leaders must adapt to the world around them, the needs of their people and the organization. The world does not stand still and neither do the organizations and people that define the world we are in. Like a plant, an organization, its culture, teams and individuals are part of and make up a living system.

A wilting organization that is nurtured by the right people, culture and innovations will resurrect. With further nourishment, the organization and its people will thrive. A thriving workplace that is neglected and deprived leads to wilting. Where nourishment is thwarted by toxicity, poor leadership and bureaucracy, it will lead to the death of the organization.

## ORGANIZATIONS AND RESILIENCE

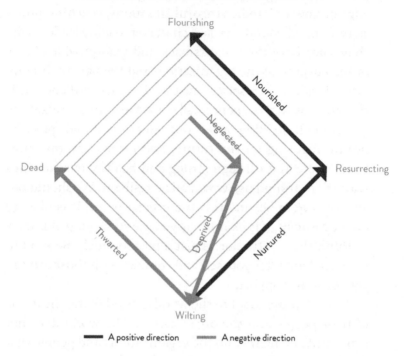

The start, the direction of travel and the ultimate destination is not a linear process for each leader, individual, team and organization. Each will go on their own journey and through their own life cycle, and with their own challenges and remedies, which ultimately determines the travel of the organization. Sometimes, it must get worse before it can get better. When an organization and its people start to wilt, the crossroad has been reached; whether the leadership and people will nurture or be thwarted will determine the next stop for the organization.

In 2021, following the coronavirus pandemic, workplaces are grappling with understanding "What's next?" There is ample talk about hybrid workstyles, yet the rhetoric is not only binary, but lacking in substance. Why is it that workstyles consistently focus on the space and place, and not the behaviours and cultures?

We have spent months hoping for an end without knowing what is coming next and I do fear what the next bit may look like for so many of us. Wellbeing has taken a battering, relationships tested, social lives non-existent, finances uncertain, jobs lost and purpose questioned.

There are many positives too. We have realized how resilient we are, we have adopted technology (even my 71-year-old Nanna is using Zoom), the amount and sheer speed of change for some organizations has been mind-blowing. People have reset themselves and remembered what is important, and the volume of remote working can only be positive for our planet.

The fact remains, the world we live in is Volatile, Uncertain, Complex and Ambiguous (VUCA) and the traditional management and leadership has little place. The US Army War College was one of the first organizations to use the VUCA acronym following 9/11, when the military were worried about the different and unfamiliar international security environment that had emerged. They used VUCA to describe it.

- → **V**olatile – change is rapid and unpredictable.
- → **U**ncertain – the present is unclear, and the future is uncertain.
- → **C**omplex – many interconnected factors create the potential to cause chaos and confusion.
- → **A**mbiguous – a lack of clarity or awareness about situations.

The biggest challenge about the world of work is that we continue to treat people as a means to an end, the vehicle for an organization to meet its financial goals.

The COVID-19 pandemic has highlighted the importance of soft skills within the workplace.[104] A survey by City and Guilds[105] found that 73% of people felt their organization's leadership had been lacking during the pandemic, 36% stating their leader failed to empower them, and 31% said a lack of empathy impacted their motivation and performance.

Before COVID-19, for many organizations, commuting and working within an office was very much the norm. Not because people genuinely wanted to be in the office and felt they worked better there but because of poor culture, mistrust and not having the technology and processes to enable people to work in a more agile way.

The 2020/2021 coronavirus pandemic reminded us all not only what is important but that there is always a better way. At the start of the pandemic, people said they did not miss the commute; four months in, the rhetoric changed to people saying they were enjoying the extra time at home with family; 12 months in, people were missing the office and not necessarily the physical space, but the belonging, connection and community.

> "Businesses that orient performance management systems around basic human needs for psychological engagement get the most out of their employees."[106]

Resilience fuels engagement. Engaging employees takes effort and commitment, but Gallup finds that when comparing businesses, those with engaged employees have higher customer satisfaction, productivity, sales and profitability and lower absenteeism, turnover, shrinkage, safety incidents and defects. The intentions and intended behaviours of engaged employees lead them to do more work.

There is not a sole answer to preparing for the future, and we will not know many of the answers to the challenges for some time; the future workplace and leadership will need to test, measure and evolve and for that approach we need resillience.

# KEY TAKEAWAYS

- It is not the job of a leader to make or break somebody. Leaders inspire, influence and impact others in order to improve performance.
- Power and control are what separate leaders and managers; managers thrive with circles of power, while leaders enable their people to thrive through circles of influence.
- We can all be human leaders, we just need to make the choice, set the intention and put the effort in.
- People do not want to be managed by a boss; they want to follow a leader, to be led by a coach.
- Human-centric leadership is not about perfection.
- Human leaders focus on team togetherness and collaboration, not individual competition and secrecy.
- A Human Leader has integrity and behaves authentically, building loyalty and trust with those around them.
- Integrity is not just one action; it is a state of mind, a way of being.
- A human-centric workplace is realistic, accepts challenges and responsibilities, is brave and embraces tough conversations, recognizing individual circumstances and approaching with empathy.
- Loyalty has little to do with length of employment or how old people are, but everything to do with actions.
- As a leader, being trustworthy is the cornerstone to motivating and inspiring and building effective and functional teams.

# REFLECTIONS

- What are your 'human' skills?
- What skills would you like to focus on improving?
- How do you show your team that you trust them?
- How can you support fellow leaders to be more human?
- Are your team loyal to you/to the organization?

## ACTIVITY: TAKE SOME TIME TO REFLECT ON YOUR STYLE OF MANAGING AND LEADING BY RATING EACH OF YOUR BEHAVIOURS ON A SCALE OF 1-10.

| 1 | 2 | 3 | 4 | 5 | 6 | 7 | 8 | 9 | 10 | Your Rating |
|---|---|---|---|---|---|---|---|---|----|-------------|

| A MANAGER | A HUMAN LEADER | |
|-----------|----------------|---|
| Builds processes | Builds people | |
| 'ME' | 'WE' | |
| Blames | Fixes | |
| Knows | Shows | |
| Takes | Gives | |
| Commands | Asks | |
| Rational | Visionary | |
| Stabilizes | Initiates change | |
| Power comes with the position | Power comes with the person | |
| Does things right | Does the right things | |
| Plans | Inspires | |
| Organizes | Influences | |
| Controls | Trusts | |
| Embraces the status quo | Challenges the status quo | |
| Documents policy | Trains and teaches | |

| 1 | 2 | 3 | 4 | 5 | 6 | 7 | 8 | 9 | 10 | Your Rating |
|---|---|---|---|---|---|---|---|---|----|-------------|

| A MANAGER | A HUMAN LEADER | |
|---|---|---|
| Follows rules | Questions the rules | |
| Execution | Ideas | |
| Risk adverse | Welcomes risk | |
| Impersonal | Emotional intelligence | |
| 'How and when?' | 'What and why?' | |
| Efficiency | Effectiveness | |
| Avoids conflict | Uses conflict to affect change | |
| Transacts | Transforms | |
| Generates fear | Earns respect | |
| Plans the details | Sets the destination | |
| Sees problems | Sees opportunities | |
| Outward focus | Self-awareness | |

## YOUR SCORE

| Score | Category | Appraisal |
|---|---|---|
| 201–270: | Human | Wow – you are absolutely rocking it. Give yourself a pat on the back and reflect on how you can support fellow leaders - keep it up! |
| 151–200: | Humanness | Great work, now look where you can focus your attention to be an even more awesome human leader |
| 101-150: | Cyborg | Reflect on how you can improve, seek a mentor and/or a coach for some support. You've got this! |
| 0–100: | Robotic | The first stage is acceptance, right? What can you do to be more human? Reflect on how you can improve, seek a mentor and/or a coach for some support. You've got this! |

# CHAPTER 5

# WAYS OF
# WORKING

Organizations and leaders face constant and mounting pressure due to the types of work arrangements and physical settings, challenges to traditional ways of working and shifting expectations from employees in line with the technologically advancing world.

Technology enables the blurring of the traditional taylorism boundaries between work and home. Where a role can be done outside of a workplace thanks to Technology, people are starting to question why working 9-5 in the same location monday-friday is neccessary. What we must take note of here is that not all roles, even with the greatest of technologies, can be done outside of a traditional workplace setting.

Pre-pandemic, many terms to define ways of working were used interchangeably, leading to confusion in organizations among both employees and employers. During the pandemic, the lingo bingo was on steroids and being captured under headlines like 'new normal' 'new ways of working' and 'reimagining the office.'

I concur with Oscar Wilde, "To define is to limit." However, without definition we have no boundaries, nothing to work to. So let us clear a few terms up:

| TERM | WHAT DOES THAT ACTUALLY MEAN? |
|------|-------------------------------|
| Agile | People work where, when and how they choose but ensure business needs are met. Technology is key to optimize performance through empowering people. |
| Office-based | Where the role is purely carried out within the workplace environment (with potential flexibility in line with company policies). |
| Remote | No people are not on a remote island, and with the exponential adoption of technology they should feel far from 'remote.' How about we stop using this term now? But if we have to define it, it should be that the person carries out a role without being dependant on an office. |
| Home worker | Where the role is carried out from a person's home environment for all or the majority of their working pattern. |
| Flexible working | A way of working that is employee-centric. Flexible start and finish times and potentially some flexibility of the location where work is carried out. |
| Activity Based Working (ABW) | People choose where to sit (or stand, or even balanced on a yoga ball) that best suits the task they are doing with the people they need to do it with. Office design and technology are crucial to ensuring mobility and experience. |
| Hot desking | This comes hand-in-hand with ABW. Where an ABW culture exists, hot desking is often the most efficient way to ensure space utilization across all settings. Hot desking gets a bad rap when it is implemented in a poor office design that leaves people fighting over a desk, or where it is implemented poorly and leaves people 'beach towelling' their favourite seat. |
| New Ways of Working (NWoW) | This is very much around organizational design and ensuring the organizational culture is brought into the current world across the whole multigenerational workforce. i.e. digital immigrants are upskilled in line with digital natives and office-based workers shift to a new way of working like agile or ABW. |
| Smart working | The approach is very much underpinned by the models of Agile and ABW and focuses on technology to improve job satisfaction and productivity. |
| Hybrid working | The 2021 trend which only time will tell if it truly is the future of work. Hybrid is about location, with many organisations favouring 3 days in the office and 2 days working from home. |

The iterations of different ways of working are not exactly radical. As my mother-in-law would say, "They are very much variations of a theme." The ways of working always come down to two things: when people work and where people work.

It is then how people work that determines what technology is required to enable the work they do, what physical spaces are required and what functionalities those spaces are facilitating.

## HYBRID WORKING

Too many organizations are still utilizing Industrial Age working styles and expecting to thrive in the information and digital age working patterns. Over recent years, there has been a surge in 'New Ways of Working' (NWoW), which ultimately focused on increasing flexibility, home-based working and desk sharing, which allowed many organizations to right size their property portfolios. For those implementing NWoW, the impacts were far reaching, with reports of better work/life balance, or alignment as wellness guru Anni Hood refers to, increases in wellbeing and productivity, financial savings, and benefits for the planet through reduced travel miles and printing. The latest and greatest way of working right for 2021 is hybrid working.

Before the pandemic lockdown, the UK had a relatively high level of occasional working at home compared with the EU average, with 18% of the workforce working at home for at least some of their working week. If we fast forward to the pandemic, in came the uppercut from COVID directly smacking corporate real estate in the chops; the percentage of those working from home increased to an average of 54%. There is little variation between sectors but, of course, there are differences between industries.[107]

The pandemic accelerated the genie escaping from the bottle and hybrid working is the talk of the town. We do appear to have become obsessed with labelling people as preferring offices or preferring working at home. But this is not a question of "ice cream or custard?" We can have both and must evolve to a way of working where people choose their location, the space and the technology they use, depending on the task they are working on, who they are working with, and what fits with their individual needs and circumstances on that day.

This is not about a free for all, by the way; that approach never has worked, and this is also not about looking at what your nearest competitor is doing. We must understand the why of your workplace – what role does the physical workplace play in enabling the organizational purpose and for people to thrive? Ways of working should not be a cookie-cutter approach across sectors, across industries, across organizations or even across departments. We must capture granular-level detail to really understand the why of the workplace and the why and how of our people, before prescribing the where.

The benefits of homeworking were overwhelmingly identified by CIPD as giving a better work/life balance (cited by 61%), followed by greater collaboration (43%), greater ability to focus with fewer distractions (38%) and IT upskilling (33%). Less widespread benefits were highlighted as enhanced health and wellbeing (20%), the ability to meet work targets (14%) and higher levels of motivation (13%).

People want the ability to have some structure and social aspects, but still independence and flexibility through a mix of the office working, home working and everything in between. There are many aspects driving employee preferences; if the home experience is a good one, then it is common sense to assume that the employee will want to continue, at least some of their working week, working from home.

There are definite generational gaps between the work setting preferences, with generation Z and millennials wanting flexibility, but the social aspects and routine that come with traditional office working, and generation X and baby boomers being more inclined to work from home for larger percentages of the week, linked to them being homeowners, care givers and living outside of the cities.

Ultimately, if the experience somebody is having in their home is better than the experience they have within the workplace, then we need to up our game. With many working from home for over a year, it has ultimately provided many with an opportunity to form a workspace that works for them; when it did not work for them, it was tweaked, something that many workplaces do not facilitate. The workplace needs to be the destination that people choose to go to, for belonging and connection, colleagues and collaboration – the things which make us human.

The destination workplace of choice is one that supports both the individual and the collaborative elements of work – communication, collaboration, contemplation and concentration. The home office will almost always be tops for privacy and avoiding interruptions, but after the pandemic way of working, we all know that collaborating in front of a screen all day soon loses its attraction, even if you do get to keep your PJs on.

Employees have their individual preferences, which must be listened to and considered during strategic planning around ways of working. Thus far, there is an expectation and experience gap between the employees' wants and needs and the employers' wants and needs.

Where organizations are in the journey toward a hybrid way of working is on a continuum of the wishful thinkers, the short termers, the seekers, and the brave and rebellious.

**The Wishful Thinkers:**

Doing nothing. Rinsing the furlough money and sitting patiently, ready for the return to 'normal'. Things surely will get better soon.

**The Seekers:**

Analysing every workplace and way of working gone before to see which the exec is most comfortable with. They are seeking permission for change.

**The Short Termers:**

Creating a COVID secure workplace so people can get back to the workplace. Let's carry on as normal.

**The Brave and Rebellious:**

The genie is out of the bottle. The workplace, workstyle and everything you stood for has been thrown upside down. You want change. You're brave. You're rebellious. You know there's a better way.

Where organizations are on the continuum is changing daily dynamically across leadership, across departments, across the people. Organizations have been left wondering what exactly the next right thing is to do. What do their people want? How are they most productive? What technology do they need? What processes need revising? Can they be productive without their manager around? Can we trust them?

The Institute of Workplace and Facilities Management (IWFM) warns that employers must act now to forge a new role for the office or risk cultural and productivity challenges. Although the global experiment can be seen as being successful, the office is not dead. Many have been left mourning the office, connection, choice and a comfy workspace set-up. Hybrid enables us to have our cake and eat it; hybrid enables the power of choice.

Between the amygdala, where conditioned fear responses are born and perpetuated, and our pre-frontal cortex, the front of our brain where we feel emotions, regulate fear and make decisions, we make hundreds of decisions every day. Despite wishful thinking, many of those decisions are not logical; even in the big decisions where we are convinced that we are being logical, the research shows that most of our decisions are made unconsciously and involve emotion.

We are faced with 11,000,000 pieces of data every second and our conscious minds cannot process all of that. Our unconscious mind has evolved to process most of the data and to make decisions for us according to guidelines and rules of thumb that are in our best interest most of the time. This is the genesis of 'trusting your gut,' and most of the time it works.

There is a neuron that fires up in the brain that triggers people to act when the brain decides it is confident of a decision. This firing up is subjective and is not necessarily based on the amount of information you have collected; it is a feeling of confidence.

Rather than just making logical arguments to persuade, you are more likely to persuade people to take an action if you understand how they are feeling about the decision and feed their feeling.

If we rewind pre-pandemic, there were so many questions and unknowns surrounding how productive people could be when working from home.

We must approach the productivity conundrum with an element of caution, although many will argue against asking employees whether they feel productive in their roles or while fulfilling certain tasks, although it is subjective, I think it is imperative to understand just exactly how people are feeling. It provides an insight into the minds of the employees. Asking employees alone should not be the only metric used to determine whether the way of working is enabling the organization's purpose and people to thrive. What is deemed productive to an employee may not be aligned to what the organization would consider productive.

Overall, organizations have seen that working from home can work for them, for most areas of the business, for at least some of the working week, and consequently executives have started to feel confident and are preparing for change.

British Council for Offices[108] found that 62% of senior executives and 58% of entry-level workers would like to divide their time between their homes and workplaces. Only 30% said they were considering returning to the office five days a week, while 15% said they would prefer to work exclusively at home.

Another survey released by Institute of Directors[109] comes to a similar conclusion, with three-quarters of respondents anticipating more homeworking after the pandemic, and more than half planning to reduce how they use physical office space in the future.

There are still organizations (the wishful thinkers) that want people back in an office five days each week; they are pushing back the changes and requesting business cases and hard facts.

As people, we like to think that we are being logical and thorough, in this instance you may need to offer logical reasons so that the person making the decision has a rational reason they can give themselves and others.

Hybrid will mean different things to different organizations, to different departments, to different leaders, to different individuals. Like any workstyle, where Hybrid is right for the people, it is right for the business.

The business case for hybrid working is building and only time will tell whether it truly is the future of work that many are claiming. The most obvious point here is that people are demanding flexibility, a new way of living. Allowing choice, freedom and showing you trust your people will drive retention levels, increase productivity, and lower hiring costs. People want to work for companies that value people.

On the productivity piece, the autonomy and trust of working where it suits the task you are doing means the individual can choose the right time, place, space and technology to maximize their productivity and give themselves a fighting chance.

With the technology available and evolving in the world right now, there is no need for many people to be in the same room every single day to collaborate.

During a period of too many online meetings, organizations are now wondering how hybrid meetings will work. What is the etiquette? How will it work in practice?

## THE ROLE OF THE CHAIR

### ALL MEETINGS:

- Before booking a meeting ask yourself, what would the consequences be of not having it?
- Be clear on what you need and want from your participants.
- Categorize meetings: Status updates / Tactical plans / Strategic long term.
- Maintain the meeting etiquette.
- Manage the size of all meeting to required participants only.
- When reviewing the agenda, where the meeting size is large, consider breaking the agenda down into smaller meetings.
- Ensure action focused notes are taken.
- Ensure notes are circulated to any absent participants.
- Start and end meetings on time.
- Engage with / check in with participants every ten minutes to ensure active engagement.

- Ensure a comfortable and psychologically safe environment where opinions can be expressed.
- Ask participants to write-up questions and go over collectively as a group. This will help those who do not feel comfortable speaking up in the moment.
- Include comfort breaks on the agenda where meetings are over one hour.
- All meetings to include a video conferencing platform link as standard.
- Be cognizant of when meetings need to be face to face and make it clear on the invite if physical attendance is preferred.
- Consider the time of day / how much notice the meeting requires and the length of the meeting.

| MEETING TYPE | IDEAL MEETING LENGTH |
| --- | --- |
| Regular team meeting | 15–30 minutes |
| Decision-making meeting | 2 hours+ depending on the decision |
| Brainstorming meeting | 45–60 minutes |
| Retrospective meeting | 30 minutes for every week in the project |
| One-to-one meeting | 30–60 minutes |
| Strategy meeting | 60–90 minutes |
| Social check-ins | 30–60 minutes |

# THE ROLE OF THE PARTICIPANT

### ALL MEETINGS:

- Take written notes, the science tells us we learn more, recollect facts better and gain a deeper understanding than when typing up notes.
- Be prepared for meetings you are attending i.e. read any pre-material and have action status updates.
- Be ready to actively engage.
- Dress appropriately in line with the meeting i.e. customer / colleague.

### WHEN ATTENDING PHYSICALLY:

- Close laptops and put phones away to avoid distractions and temptation.
- Do not start side chats during the meeting, ensure virtual participants are included.
- If the use of a whiteboard is required, utilize the virtual board to ensure virtual participants are included.

### WHEN ATTENDING VIRTUALLY:

- Close your email inbox, mute any notifications, and close any documents/windows not relevant to the meeting.
- Use a headset to improve sound quality and mute yourself when you are not talking.
- Turn your camera on. It helps to have non-verbal cues, facial expressions humanize meetings, seeing people forges relationships and also reduces the temptation to multitask.
- Use the 'raise your hand' functionality and utilize the chat function to comment/ask a question without speaking. Note, please do not use the chat function to have side chats.
- Avoid sitting in front of a bright window as your colleagues will struggle to see your face.

Social connectivity, mental health, physical health and technology and tools available will determine productivity, not the physical space.

There is a battle for talent. Hybrid working not only increases the potential talent pool in relation to commuting distances, but by being a leader, an organization, a business, that people want to work for will increase both recruitment and retention rates.

Desk working costs thousands in rent, business rates, service charges, insurance, lighting, cooling, and heating, space management, facilities management resources. With the right data, the right amount of data, at the right time, hybrid working models will allow organizations to right size, repurpose or reimagine their physical spaces.

COVID aside, we all know at least one person who crawls into the office clinching a box of tissues and wearing their germs like a badge of honour. For the record, when it comes to germs in an office, sharing is not caring. There are some illnesses (physical and mental) that may mean somebody can work, but not work within an office environment. A hybrid way of working will enable germs to be kept away from the office or for an individual to take some time out, without necessarily them taking a whole day off. However, having the right culture and data is crucial to ensuring people are not burning themselves out when their body is crying out for a day of rest.

Now, I know my friends in Canada will laugh at this but, when it snows in the UK, it suddenly becomes absolute bedlam. If so many of us can work at home during a pandemic, how about the next time it snows we act a little more sensibly and just stay at home if the roads and infrastructure do not allow us to travel to work safely and efficiently?

On the point of travel, hybrid working will reduce the amount of unnecessary travel undertaken. Not just cars on the road, but the executives who fly around the world for a meeting.

On the surface, you would think that hybrid working is an obvious choice for the future workplace. However, hybrid will not work for everybody and needs to be approached with some caution. Hybrid is not right for everybody and every organization. Choose what is right for your organization, the people who drive it and the people you serve. Ask your people, collect data, measure and evolve. Avoid the kneejerk and the following of trends.

There were many surveys during the pandemic, and although we can take the data to inform what the future world may look like for us all, we must be wary of using data collected during a pandemic, with home schooling, strains on Wi-Fi, a lack of or sharing of devices, anxieties, full lock downs and no social interaction, the fact that all of this went on for a long time and of course, let us not forget that for many, home working became a quick decision out of necessity.

We can and should use the data to help inform what next looks like. We need to continue the data collection, apply trends to our organizations and people, and give hybrid working a true and fair test under more controlled, planned and, most importantly, balanced conditions. One size does not fit all.

Some jobs cannot simply be done working from home. I do not mean the jobs where technology/trust/new systems will enable home working. I mean the jobs where I would prefer my surgeon to be in the room.

It is also the case that some people can simply not work from home. Not because of the tasks they are doing but because of mental health and wellbeing, the need for interaction, the need for escapism from home life or the need to simply learn from others closely around them.

Reducing the property footprint is a concept that has become synonymous with hybrid working. I would advise you to be cautious before starting to implement lease breaks, until you know how your people want to work and that they are enabled to do so, physically, culturally and technologically. Collate data to compare the intended use of the workplace versus the actual use of the workplace and even then, first assess if the workplace can be repurposed rather than removed.

For hybrid to be successful, your organization will need a trusting and open culture. Is your culture, leaders, technology and systems ready – are they human-centric workplace ready?

There's always that person who sends an email and then walks to your desk to tell you they sent an email. In a hybrid world, we are at risk of some people creating their own cultures and venting frustrations at the slowness of reply. A human-centric workplace respects all people and endorses clarity and discussion over gossip and bitching.

The ability to turn and ask a quick question, watch somebody carry out a task, build workplace relationships and be mentored are all crucial for workplace learning and development. Who do your inexperienced team members learn from and how? How will you ensure the development of your people?

Leaders, your people need support. Pandemic or not, we all have struggles with balance, boundaries, responsibilities and a lack of routine.

Flexible working policies, agile mindsets and activity-based working while utilizing smart technology covers the all-important people, process, space and technology to ensure your people can thrive.

**Flexible Working
Policies**

**Activity Based
Working**

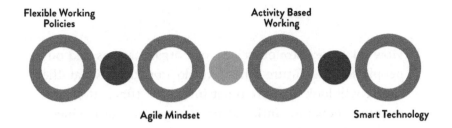

**Agile Mindset**

**Smart Technology**

UK Data Service[110] found that 9.3% of workers – equivalent to three million people – said they would prefer to work shorter hours and accept the cut in pay that comes with this. Working 9-to-5, barely getting by, all talk and no giving, people using your mind without giving the credit ... well, Dolly was right, it is enough to drive us crazy if we let it.

We must embrace flexibility, full throttle. Where people work is sometimes outside of anybody's control, but when and how we work is generally for grabs.

Despite the initial panic following the mass exodus out of the workplace, thanks to the hard work of the workplace ninjas, technology, conscious leadership and a ton of resilience, the world is functioning; the impossible has become workable.

There is a space in your employee experience for the workplace and its an important space that needs to be used to drive connectedness, collaboration and belonging.

We have been presented with a once-in-a-lifetime opportunity to reimagine work and the workplace. We need to grab hold of it tight, take the learnings and focus on the recovery. Our people need our focus to enable them to recover from what, for so many, has been a traumatic and stressful period. Engage your people, enable them through ways of working and technology and evolve through data. The workstyle of the organisation should be human-centric and drive your organisation forward.

# BE FUTURE READY

How do we prepare ourselves, our organizations and our people for the future when we do not know what the future will look like? We must invest the time, effort and resources now into anticipating changes in your business, your markets and wider society.

Having our 'why' keeps us focused, makes us dig deep during tough times, coming up with creative solutions to get one step closer. As Nietzsche wrote over one hundred years ago, one who has a 'why' to live for can endure almost any 'how.' People want to do meaningful work, and organizations need to ensure they have their clearly defined purpose outlined so every single person and function understands what their contribution means to the bigger picture.

People do not like uncertainty. We need to ensure that ourselves, our people and the organizations have clarity, that our purpose is aligned and communications are strong.

In a dispersed world, organizational culture needs intentional, conscious and consistent effort to maintain and be built on; it is a crucial competitive advantage. Take time to understand what your organization's DNA is and how it is reflected, lived and breathed day-to-day.

We build our people and in return they build our business. Future leaders need to be skilled at the hard stuff – the 'soft' stuff: trust, psychological safety, empathy, authenticity and vulnerability.

Strong leadership is required to ensure your people and organization are future ready. To drive your team and organization into the future, you must have solid foundations, trust, listening, empathy, and the gift of giving and receiving feedback. Remember that every choice, every action, has a result and you may not see that result straight away;

be present and intentional with your choices and actions. Listen to your team, ask what is and is not working.

You know what you get from sitting on the fence don't you? Splinters. Be brave, act, make things happen, fail, learn and try again! Just get the sh*t done. We need to fail and bounce back stronger, reinventing, innovating and consistently solving problems. Promoting a culture of creativity and embracing mistakes gives your people freedom to think outside the box and fail, and will enable your people to overcome the toughest of challenges. At a macro-organizational level, leaders need to keep an eye on trends, learn from others and stay at the forefront of their sector.

Hearts and minds must be brought along the journey; leaders need to model the values of the organization. Not the values just written on the wall; the ones that your people truly live and breathe – the behaviours. Do the values and behaviours of the organization need revisiting? How do you ensure your people are engaged and connected to the purpose of the organization? Nobody is exempt; people need to see people of all levels in the organizations living and breathing values and embracing change.

The flatter the hierarchy, the more agile and collaborative the organization. An important part of designing for adaptability and resilience is a shift away from hierarchical organizational structures toward models where work is accomplished in teams. To be future ready, the organization must foster a mindset of collaboration, transparency and innovation between such key supporting departments of the organization. Too often, Facilities, IT and HR work in silos despite having the shared end goal of being being an enabler of the people and therefore driver of the business. Rapport and strength of relationships gets stuff done; people dig deep for each other.

In teams, accountability becomes more transparent. Individual and team goals and metrics should be shared for everyone to see. The sense of accountability this can create is critical to team and corporate effectiveness. This, of course, links to rapport and relationships; digging deep together as a team.

Speed, agility and adaptability are crucial – siloed and top-down organizations based on predictable commercial events are a thing of the past. The unpredictability and disruption need speed, agility and adaptability to stay ahead. There will be more ambiguity, and we need to embrace that and be comfortable not knowing what is coming next.

The world is moving quickly; organizations need to anticipate change and find quick solutions to problems through creativity, collaboration and curiosity. Speed, agility, adaptability and ambiguity require curiosity. The more curious we are, the more information we have, the more we can connect the dots at speed. The way we do things now got us to the here and now, it does not mean the same ways will be fit and functional to get us to whatever is coming next over the horizon. There is always a better way; find out what that better way is and do it.

On a personal level, remember that time is precious. Imagine what you could do with 450 hours at work or in your homelife; if you waste just 15 minutes every day for five years, that is 450 hours you are not getting back. Take time to reflect, to clear your mind and untangle things, slow down so you can speed up. Curiosity may have killed the cat, but what kind of life would the cat have lived if it had avoided curiosity? Be curious, ask questions, ask why, keep learning, do not settle, and find solutions to the problems effecting you, your team, the organization and wider society.

The final points on being future ready concern the physical spaces and technology. They need to be true enablers for the organization through facilitating mobility, connection and collaboration.

The physical spaces need to enable different ways of working, agility and collaboration. There will be a need for increased collaboration spaces, streamlined ways to book spaces, enhanced storage, improved AV technology, a way of providing visitors with a 'wow' first and lasting impression and ensuring that the spaces cater for the needs of its users.

Too many organizations continually try to fit the people to the spaces, instead of the spaces to the people. Whether it be the square footage, the design or the functionality, space is an enabler for people to get sh*t done, to thrive as individuals and as team players to ultimately drive organizational goals.

How about we stop planning working patterns on the size of the space, but the need of the individual/team/organization? And how about we stop putting our heads in our hands when people do not use the space as we intended and work out what needs to change? The physical space needs to be a destination people want and enjoy going to.

For your people and organization to be successful in this dispersed working world that we are in, we must ensure that the collaboration tools and the technology platforms are a fit for the work that is being done. For example, meeting rooms need to be good enough that everybody feels seen and heard no matter if they are in the room or working outside of the office – no more silhouettes, no more crackly connections and no more side conversations.

This also applies to hardware; nobody wants to work from home if it means lumping a 10kg laptop around with them that they would just love to throw out of the window. Processes need to be slick and documents accessible from anywhere. No more ring binders and dull grey filing cabinets.

People must have clarity in understanding which environment is best suited to the work that we are doing; through empowering our people and giving them autonomy and trust to choose which environment that they feel they will work best in, our people will thrive thus our organizations will thrive.

It is time to reassess life. I know, deep, right? But there is nothing like a pandemic to make us all feel off-kilter and in need of stepping back and re-evaluating. I have absolutely been guilty of spreading myself too thin, not saying no, taking on too much, wishing there were an extra few hours in each day to do things that did not even make me feel alive, and ultimately did not fit in with my values and purpose. The pandemic allowed many, including myself, to decide they would never go back to their old normal.

Measure, refine, deliver, repeat. Focus on continuous improvement and marginal gains. Adopt continuous, feedback-based performance management; regular feedback empowers people to reset goals continuously, change projects and feel rewarded for their 'work,' not just their 'job.' Employee survey tools give managers immediate input on their own performance, boosting transparency.

> "In our generation, the struggle of whether we connect more, whether we achieve our biggest opportunities, comes down to this – your ability to build communities and create a world where every single person has a sense of purpose."[111]

It is time to press the reset button on our lives:

→ Eating breakfast with the kids and taking them to school.
→ More sleep.
→ More exercise.

→ Loading the dishwasher during a quick stretch of the legs and resting of the eyes.

→ Avoiding the dreaded sorting office or the guessing of where certain parcel couriers have dumped your parcels by having the ability to answer the door.

→ Working in the garden on the four days a year the UK has some sun.

→ Walking the dog during your lunch break.

→ Going to the doctor without booking half a day's holiday.

→ Eating fresh (and much cheaper!) food from your own fridge.

→ Drinking the coffee that you like.

→ Opening a window (until your neighbour mows their lawn!).

→ Controlling the heating from your phone.

→ Knowing that the work you do matters.

→ Feeling a sense of belonging, a community.

→ Being conscious of not just our effect on others, but on the planet.

Look after your people and they will look after you. None of this is about new and different ways of working, but about new ways of living.

## KEY TAKEAWAYS

- Our workstyles and behaviours have a wider impact. Stop forcing people to commute for an hour to sit in an office every day. Enable change.
- We can do better, and we must do better, for the sake of our people, our organizations and our planet.
- The way an organisation chooses to work must be chosen for the right reasons; to enable people to drive the business forward. Understand the 'why' before the 'what' and the 'how'.

# REFLECTIONS

- How do your people want to work?
- What is working and what is not?
- How do we create a fulfilling and equitable experience for all?
- How do you foster a culture in which leaders see it as their responsibility to design and execute social-connectivity practices for their teams?
- When employees work remotely, how do you replicate the ad hoc, serendipitous encounters with colleagues who work on the same team or were once down the hallway?
- How do you maintain team cohesion when some people are working remotely while others are onsite?
- What steps should you take to help employees manage the blurring of work-life boundaries and the cognitive overload from being digitally engaged all day?
- What benefits, incentives and structures might you put in place to encourage wellbeing?
- What digital tools do employees need in a non-office-centric workplace – particularly to support collaborative tasks?
- What role does the company play in either providing the physical tools and equipment needed to work from home, such as external monitors and ergonomic chairs, or compensating employees so that they can purchase them?
- When part of the team is in the office and part of it is at home, how do you develop norms to ensure that everyone feels included?
- What does your organization want and need to use the office for?

# CHAPTER 6

# A PLACE WHERE PEOPLE THRIVE

Okay, let's talk space. If you looked at the contents page, initially you may have been wondering why a book about creating workplaces where people thrive has saved the chapter about the physical space until this late in the book, but hopefully, as the previous chapters have highlighted, workplaces are about people; the space just had to get in line.

When most roles could only be done in one place, life was uncomplicated. 'Work' was somewhere you went for your contracted time and you were paid for the hours worked. Now life is more complex. For many, technology has liberated work from the constraints of a fixed place and given the worker the feeling of choice over when to perform it. 'Work' is no longer a place we go; it is an activity, a set of tasks, for a given purpose. With strategies and key performance indicators, work is a process for achieving results – it is the output that matters. And yet, the average worker is still paid for their input, not their output, leading to presenteeism and the work shy going under the radar because they are visible and, therefore, they must be working.

For people to thrive, we must understand their needs as humans, how the brain works, how you as a leader can impact and influence, the importance of culture, the beauty of integrity, loyalty and trust, the many ways of working that get the work done and yes, people need space to do the work in. And that space can be almost anywhere where technology enables (even some trains, if you have a bit of patience).

Space is only one facet that makes up the workplace.

## Workplace = People + Space + Technology

The when and the how we work is up for grabs, but where people work is sometimes outside of anybody's control. The workplace where people thrive is the workplace that is a destination people want to go to; it is physical, virtual or a mix of both.

Gone are the days of 'the bigger the better' and despite the resistance from some, the corner office with the big mahogany desk, well, in their heads it may still form part of their identity and power play, but I am afraid that is where the necessity ends.

I have seen thousands of workplaces. I have walked into some workplaces and felt warm inside (the comfy feeling, not the temperature, may I add), welcomed, connected, inspired and almost envious that I did not work there. I have walked into other workplaces and genuinely felt drained, warm (the actual temperature), grubby and angry. Angry that human beings must work there, when if bringing dogs was an option, I would opt out to save her from such a drab experience.

As the inspirational Neil Usher highlights, firstly creating a fantastic workplace is simple with a bit of simple sense, and secondly, a fantastic workplace is attainable with collective apprehension.[112] When somebody of Neil's experience and insight declares this, my sense of hope for all our futures is refuelled.

When we come away from the gimmicks, scrolling through Pinterest boards and looking at what your nearest competitor is doing, and instead put the needs of your people at the heart of the workplace, to enable people to bring their human – that is when workplaces are created where people thrive.

When putting the needs of your people at the heart of the workplace, there are some key questions to consider:

→ What is the purpose of the workplace?
  (Why are people there?)
→ How do people behave within the workplace?
  (What is the culture?)
→ What does the physical space look and feel like?
  (The design, the vibe.)

→ What technology and tools are in place?
(Are they enabling or frustrating?)
→ How is employee experience measured?
(Do people want to be there?)
→ How is effectiveness and efficiency measured?
(Is it a cost or a value?)

## PURPOSE

The purpose of the physical workplace has drifted and evolved over the years and, at times, for some organizations, the purpose has been certainly lacking. The pandemic made us question the purpose of the physical workplace more than ever after the virtual world really upped the ante. The workplace is both physical and virtual and has been for quite some time for many. The pandemic was the accelerant for something which we all knew deep down – the way we work is not working for us.

In March 2020, the UK entered the first national lock-down due to COVID-19. As a Workplace Consultant I was certainly busy, not with the physical offices, but preparing people for change, the change that had arrived that brought with it home working, uncertainty and, for some, a hack job to get people out of the offices and set-up working from home quickly. There were many working at the kitchen table. I had one friend who was balancing her laptop on an ironing board, another who made a standing desk by adding a cardboard box to the kitchen worktop.

As the weeks and months went on, there were challenges; we were in the same storm, but there were many different boats. I will apply my own personal challenges to the 12 Elements of the Workplace.[113]

| 1 **Da** Daylight | | | | 2 **Co** Connectivity |
|---|---|---|---|---|
| 3 **Sp** Space | 4 **Ch** Choice | 5 **In** Influence | 6 **Cn** Control | 7 **Re** Refresh |
| 8 **Se** Sense | 9 **Cf** Comfort | 10 **Ic** Inclusion | 11 **Wa** Wash | 12 **St** Storage |

Wait ... before you read on, let me caveat this: I am aware that throughout the COVID-19 pandemic, I was in a privileged position. I was not working for the NHS, I was not on furlough, my job felt secure, I was not home schooling, and I had a home office fully set-up for remote working in a safe environment.

→ Daylight: In the summer it was blinding. In the winter I had to resort to a selfie light attached to the top of my monitor to avoid being on calls looking like I was in a cave with a torch under my chin.

→ Connectivity: Everything was fine with the broadband as long as my wife and I did not need to be on a video conferencing call at the same time. Month one, I bought a wireless keyboard and mouse. Month two, I bought a second monitor. Month three, my laptop broke, and I did a 200-mile roundtrip to an office to get it sorted. All in all, no major issues.

→ Space: I was one of the lucky ones who had a home office designed just as I wanted; unlike my wife, who was plonked at the kitchen table for months on end (for the record, I did offer to share my space).

→ Choice: During summer, the choice was most delightful. I worked in the garden, in a park and did a lot of walking calls with my headphones in. The winter was a different matter, if I had stayed in my office chair any longer, I think the fibres would have fused me there forever.

→ Influence: I love my office, I have decorated it just how I want it, I change it to suit and often have work stuck up on the wall; after all, it is my home.

→ Control: In the summer, having the windows open was great until a neighbour mowed their lawn. In the winter, I was very aware of the heating being on a lot (not as aware as my wife; she is from Yorkshire, make of that what you will!). In the end, a quick purchase of a fan kept me going through the summer and a newly installed phone app to control the heating kept me going during the latter winter months. Noise was the biggest issue, if it was not lawnmowers, leaf blowers or a drill, it was my neighbour's lockdown puppy yapping. The do not disturb function on my instant messaging platform at least saved me from some interruptions.

→ Refresh: There were days when back-to-back calls left me gasping, but at least when I did get a drink it was exactly the coffee I wanted to drink. On the days where diaries would align and I could eat lunch with my wife, that was nice.

→ Sense: I enjoyed working in a space where I had chosen the colour and the scent, well, there were no strange smells wafting from the microwave, which was a lovely change from the usual daily grind.

→ Comfort: In a world where it was dangerous to be within 2m of another person, being in my own home with my wife and dog meant I genuinely could not have been anymore comfy.

→ Wash: There was not a millimetre of space that was not covered in some form of antibacterial property. As for the bathroom, well, my office is right next door to it, so there were advantages when you only had a 30-second gap between meetings, and disadvantages when the wife slams the bathroom door when you are in the middle of a call.

→ Storage: I had a pedestal full of stationary, just how I like it.

So yes, overall, I was in a privileged position. However, I do think it is important that as humans we should not compare our emotions, experiences and positions to others; otherwise, we would either be never good enough or living a life full of guilt. I experienced my own challenges. I do not want to compare, they were my challenges, my feelings, my experiences and I will not dimmish them.

I worked awfully long days (10–13 hours), sitting in the same room staring at a screen. I suffered from insomnia, anxiety, low mood and cabin fever. My wife broke her ankle and with that came a whole wave of emotions and challenges. And even though I am an introvert, I missed people. Like everybody, I was worried about my friends, my family, my neighbours, my community, the whole world.

As each of the waves of COVID-19 passed, the chatter about reopening workplaces began in earnest. I remember saying to a colleague, "The longer this goes on, the more the world of work will look different when it is all over."

Employers were implementing or at least planning for one-way systems, temperature checks, plexiglass screens, tape, signage, increased cleaning, health screening and ways to reduce risk of spreading the virus.

At the same time, there was a parallel conversation taking place: why do we need to return to an office?

The unthinkable became reality and, although cobbled together, it was working for the majority.

Although my needs in relation to the 12 elements of the workplace were being met, something was just not right, and it was not just the fact that we were in a global pandemic and I was working too many hours. Like many, I missed the office, and despite speaking to my colleagues more than ever, I missed them, I missed being in the office with them. The cognitive dissonance of our minds being connected but not our bodies. The spontaneous chats, their body language, bumping into a colleague from a different department on the way to the toilet, going for lunch and just the general sense of community and belonging when your tribe are all in the same physical space and you can see the whites of their eyes.

The virtual workplace certainly has its attractions, but we must get better at organizing our days, we must find balance and variety, not just in the location we work, but the ways we work. This ability to work anywhere is both a blessing and a curse for the employee; we have to all learn how to manage the blurred boundaries between home and work. We must find our new way of living that suits us as individuals, as teams, as organizations, as a planet.

The constant barrage of virtual meetings is draining. Stanford[114] was one of the first to examine the psychological consequences of spending hours per day in virtual meetings and found four key impacts: 1) Excessive amounts of close-up eye contact is highly intense, 2) Seeing yourself during video chats is fatiguing, 3) Video chats reduce our usual mobility, and 4) The cognitive load is much higher in video chats.[115] To add a fifth point to this, if people were in a physical meeting and took a second to think, you would pick up the cues and be comfortable; in the video conferencing world, when there is silence, you feel instant anxiety and automatically check that your Wi-Fi has not frozen.

The virtual world leaves us wanting for more. The asynchronous way of working, the small talk, the laughter, the overpriced coffee, a handshake, a hug. The feeling of the company culture by being in a space, together, with colleagues, the sense of belonging, collaborating, innovating, problem solving. The routine and certainty. Just because we can do a video chat does not mean we have to for every single meeting. There is now something quite delightful about a good old fashioned phone call, and if we get our focus right, there will also be something equally delightful about in-person meetings – honest.

The pendulum has swung too far, and the next few years ahead will find it calibrating somewhere in the middle. For the majority, there is still a need and a desire for a physical workplace, but that workplace needs to be a destination that people want to go to and the 'why' must be clear. People will go to a workplace where they see the benefit of that reason for themselves, their colleagues or the organization. They will no longer accept going to a workplace on the basis that their mere presence is a trigger for the command-and control style of leadership.

> "The business of people talking to each other in offices is a very serious consideration. It is by far the most expensive achievement of offices: the grouping of people that allows conversational exchange."[116]

Propst[116] profoundly highlighted that although "office work has undergone a revolution; the physical environment lags behind," he observed that workers had multiple responsibilities, but these were not being supported by multiple workstations.

Given that Propst was raising the point of flexibility and activity-based working back in 1968, and 50 years later, in 2018, Neil Usher highlighted that creating a fantastic workplace is simple and attainable – why have we not kind of, you know, just got on with it by now? We know what to do and why we need to do it, but I am not sure whether many know where to start and I am not sure many are ready to just let go of the power and status which the physical office has reflected, fuelled and enforced for such a long time.

Workplaces live on, physically and virtually. There is no one size fits all; creating a workplace where people can thrive is going to need conscious leadership, effort, listening, communication, an open mind, humility and empathy. We need to bring our human and empower others to bring theirs. We must remain connected and driven by our why – what is the workplace for? What is the physical workplace enabling? How is the virtual world utilized?

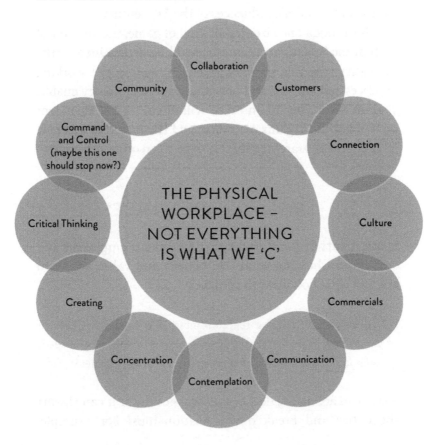

THE PHYSICAL
WORKPLACE –
NOT EVERYTHING
IS WHAT WE 'C'

Collaboration

Community

Customers

Command
and Control
(maybe this one
should stop now?)

Connection

Critical Thinking

Culture

Creating

Commercials

Concentration

Communication

Contemplation

Despite the calls of "the office is dead," I believe the office is just getting started and that in the coming years, we will truly start to appreciate and understand the purpose and wonderfulness that comes with a physical workplace, at least for some of our working week, and certainly not all of it, as long as our roles, culture, space, technology and processes allow.

The power is in our hands to redefine the future workplace, but we must act now. COVID-19 has accelerated much-needed and long overdue change. This is not about what the purpose of the office is and new ways of working, this is about what the purpose of our lives is and new ways of living. We can finally achieve a model of work that has adapted to the social, technological and economic influences of the 21st century.

This is not a one-size-fits-all kind of game, the amount of each of the "C's" done in an office will be determined by the individual, the role they do, neurodivergence, the working practices and culture, and how space and technology enable. The ultimate 'why' of an office will of course be dependent upon what the organization does and the part that you play in it, but the overarching reason to go to an office is people.

## HUMAN-CENTRIC PLACES

Space is part of the story being told to your employees and customers, showing what you believe and value, who you are and what you want to achieve.

"Consciously or not, we feel and internalize what space tells us about how to work. When you walk into most offices, the space tells you that it's meant for a group of people to work alone."[117]

Space can accelerate deeper cultural bonds, or it can thwart those ties and break down relationships. For example, organizations moving toward transparency and collaboration would need to reduce any physical signs of hierarchy such as private offices.

"Space matters. We read our physical environment like we read a human face."[118] Our space informs the way we work, how we interact with each other and how we behave.

When putting the needs of your people at the heart of the workplace, the culture of the organization needs to be reflected within the physical space. In return, the physical space can and does drive and determine behaviours and plays a significant role in shaping the experience.

Too many organizations continually try to fit the people to the spaces instead of the spaces to the people, whether it be the square footage, the design or the functionality. Buildings are simple to manage until you put people in them and turn them into workplaces, but without the people, a building has no purpose.

Space is an enabler for people to get sh*t done, to thrive as individuals and as team players, to ultimately drive organizational goals.

How about we stop planning working patterns on the size of the space, but the need of the individual/team/organization? How about we stop seeing the workplace as a capital expenditure, budgeted for every 5–10 years, and how about we stop putting our heads in our hands when people do not use the space as we intended, and instead work with the people who are experiencing the challenges, and find out what needs to change and why?

Of course, we should guide behaviours in the workplace, utilizing Nudge Theory[119] to initiate new behaviours or shape existing ones. But if managing your workplace is like herding cats, there is something wrong with it either culturally, physically or technologically. I often see nudges used incorrectly, used more of a rule to incentivize or punish behaviour. Remember that nudges are meant to be indirect, not direct enforcement or instructions. The nudge concept should instil freedom of choice but enable people to make better decisions; the softly-softly approach is more successful than a heavy-handed approach to mandating behaviour change. Take time to understand challenges and gently nudge people to new behaviours.

Examples of nudges in spaces include: smaller crockery in the canteen (people eat less), removing waste bins from the desks (less waste, more exercise), central staircases and lifts tucked away (stairs become the default for those physically able), centrally located tea points (to aid casual encounters), fewer printers (less printing, more exercise), healthy snacks at eye level (healthy choices), sit/stand desks (less sitting, more standing), arrows/footstep vinyls (nudge people toward a desired route) and standing collaboration areas (shorter meetings).

Through taking a design thinking approach to our spaces, involving the users and taking feedback from a variety of vantage points, organizations can address the real needs of the space that go far beyond the cookie-cutter approach that currently happens, and drive the level of employee experience that is going to be needed to ensure the workplace becomes a destination your people want to go to, and if people treat the space as you intended, then it is a win-win all round.

The fit-out industry probably will not appreciate me saying this, but it needs saying. There are far too many companies that complete fit-outs and judge the success on whether they are contacted again in another five years or not, and they are giving the sector a bad rap. The world is advancing at speed, and our workplaces need to continually evolve; the feast-and-famine approach is short sighted and too rigid. Through approaching workplaces with a mindset of constant evolution, little and often, workplaces can be that destination that people want to go to.

Decision makers, please stop setting budgets and timescales and then asking contractors to design the art of the impossible. Creating a destination that people want to go to does not start with design.

The Human Workplace is one that evolves with the needs and desires of the people in their quest to meet the organization's mission, it requires curiosity, empathy, grit, determination, patience and a whole load of listening.

**THE 12-STEP JOURNEY**

## PHASE 1: DISCOVERY

"If the brief looks like a design, it is a design and you have not created a brief. Go back."[120]

Well, I cannot argue with that. Taking time now to discover what is happening in the here and now will save you a world of pain and cost in the future, ensuring the spaces are exactly what people require to do their roles and reflect the culture of the organization.

1. Collate data: Employee engagement, space utilization, sickness and absence, head count, employee retention and churn rates, predicted growth, NPS, helpdesk ticket trends and any other form of data relevant to your organization.
2. Understand what the current trends are, what competitors are doing for their people and their workplaces, and the challenges they come up against.
3. The voice of the people: using the data collated, how are people feeling? What do they want? What do they need? Dig deeper with specific surveys, interviews and focus groups.

## PHASE 2: VISION

"To the person who does not know where he wants to go there is no favourable wind." – Seneca

An articulated vision will give direction, inspire the opportunities for innovation, unify, engage and energize the stakeholders. The workplace needs focus and a clear purpose.

4. The art of the possible: what does the organization want the future to look like?

5. Budget: what can the organization spend on delivering the art of the possible? The approach of the human workplace is one that sees value, not costs.
6. Timescales: when does the project start and end?

**PHASE 3: DETAIL**

"The devil is in the details." – Nietzsche

This is where the discovery and the vision combine, bringing together the desires, the viability and the feasibility. What does the data say about the workplace now and what does the organization say about what the workplace needs to be in the future, and how can we make it happen?

7. RAID: Risks, Assumptions, Issues, Dependencies.
   RACI: Responsible, Accountable, Consulted, Informed.
8. Workshops: Ideation and visualization = mind maps, sketches, photo montages and mood boards.
9. Design: Design renders/virtual walk-throughs.

**PHASE 4: IMPLEMENT**

"Vision without action is a dream. Action without vision is simply passing the time. Action with vision is making a positive difference."[121]

Right, enough talking – now, it is time to get started on the implementation. Show your people you have listened, learned, reflected and are ready to give them the workplace that enables them to thrive.

10. Pilot the design.
11. Measure: go back to the users – what is working, what is not working, what would they change?

12. Mindset: and so it begins again. You work is not done. This is a cycle; you are now back to collecting organization data.

## THE EMPLOYEE EXPERIENCE

The battle for the heart and the mind of employees is played out every single day on a global scale in the mission to drive experience and sustain competitive advantage. Such experience is impacted by the culture of the organization, from leadership, trust and psychological safety, wellbeing, and career progression and simply having a friend at work. The spaces we work in, the technology that enables (or hinders) and the processes we follow to get work done in a way the organization requires.

Employees need to know what part they play in the organization, that they belong and the reasons why, the reasons their work matters, and why they as an individual matter.

As humans, to truly be happy, we will always need something more. Neuroscientist Jaak Panksepp argued that of seven core instincts in the human brain (anger, fear, panic-grief, maternal care, pleasure/lust, play and seeking), seeking is the most important.[122]

The human seeking system, fuelled by dopamine, is linked to how humans plan activities, meaning humans are rewarded with a surge of dopamine for exploring what is 'next.' This does not mean that we will never be happy; it simply means that we will always be seeking – it is the seeking that makes us happy.

When I understood the seeking system, I understood why my friend consistently looks for new houses, even though they are perfectly happy where they live. Why even when I have been happy at work, I sometimes cannot refrain from having a look at the job market and the phrase, "money cannot buy everything" suddenly resonated too. People will always seek; the innate human yearning to seek means that we can never genuinely feel that every desire and wish has been met. There will always be something on our to-do list, and it is this fact that makes life fulfilling.

People seek, and if the experience is not a good one, if they do not feel gratitude, when they find something that they perceive to be a better experience, temptation will kick in and they will go elsewhere. The better the employee experience is, the more connected they are to the purpose and their colleagues, the more they care, their efforts increase, the better people perform and the chance of temptation kicking in lessens.

If you do not measure it, you form an opinion, not a fact, and you do not know what needs to change, why or how. Key measures of employee experience include:

- Surveys to capture trends.
- Space data – are the workplace 'perks' such as the onsite gym being used?
- Do your employees refer their friends/family to work for your organization?
- What is the employee churn rate?
- What are sickness levels like in comparison to national or sector averages? Are there certain departments with higher sickness levels?
- How many internal promotions has there been year-on-year?
- One-to-ones to capture honest feedback and workshops to focus on solutions.
- Benchmarking – what are your rivals doing? What awards are they winning? What are they blogging about on social media?

Use a mix of the measures noted and ensure qualitative and quantitative data is collated. You may find benefit in engaging with a third party to assist you in assessing and building your employee experience. With a third party comes well-rounded experiences of different organizations and markets, impartiality, a fresh set of eyes and a nod to your employees that you are investing in their experience and taking it seriously.

## EXPERIENCE/EFFECTIVENESS/ EFFICIENCY

I have always been somewhat perplexed by the approach to real estate that many larger organizations take. There is either too much space, in preparation for growth, or not enough space, leaving the organization on the hunt for space in the proximity of the existing location. Either way, it is an inefficient and ineffective use of real estate and incurs higher direct and indirect costs. If there is too much space, employees can feel lost, disconnected, ghosttown-like. If there is too little space, employees feel like battery hens, not cared for, frustrated and verging on feeling claustrophobic.

Employee experience comes, quite literally, before effectiveness and efficiency. It is all good and well making things efficient, financially, but if it affects employee experience, and it will bite you on the backside later down the line.

Post-COVID-19, larger organizations are looking to downsize their corporate real estate on the premise that hybrid working means less desks are required in an office, resulting in spikes in hot desking and the technologies to book spaces. Pre-pandemic, those organizations who collated data on their spaces, overall, certainly showed they had ample space; however, a lot of organizations had no space utilization data and little understanding of how their spaces were being utilized or why. Hybrid working should not be associated with downsizing; it should be associated with repurposing space, so it enables the employee experience.

A workplace that is efficient, in space utilization terms, does not mean it is efficient for the people, which consequently hits the finances of the organization. The workplace is an enabler for people to thrive and therefore the organization to thrive and, as such, mindsets need to shift away from costs per square foot to value per square foot.

What square footage is needed to create a workplace that is the vehicle for people to thrive and deliver the organization's goals is individual to the organization and its people. There is a tightrope that needs to be walked to gain a happy medium between experience, effectiveness and efficiency and too often efficiency is overpowering to the detriment of effectiveness and experience.

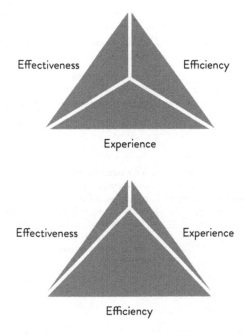

To walk the tightrope, organizations need to weigh up which operating model they pursue:

| OPERATING MODEL | WHAT IS IT? | THE BENEFITS | THE CHALLENGES |
|---|---|---|---|
| Traditional lease | Space let to a business owner by its landlord for a certain period – anything between 1 and 15 years. | Control over how you use and manage your spaces. The business has the space to evolve and establish the culture within the space. In comparison, the costs longer term are lower. Security and certainty of the lease terms – length and rental costs. | Often high Capex for an initial fit-out, plus reinstatement/dilapidation costs at lease end. The space needs managing. The business is responsible for arranging utilities and pays rates and service charges of which they have little control over. Growth needs to be forecasted fairly accurate as the square footage is fixed for the duration of the lease term. If you are a younger company, the landlord often expects a large deposit to satisfy any perceived risks of you defaulting on payment. |
| Landlord | The owner of the real estate. | Complete control of the space. A potential income stream. Capital growth. | The initial financial expense. Legal responsibilities. Building management required to maintain state of repair. Property valuation risks. Dilapidations and Capex. |
| Coworking / Space as a Service (Sp-a-a-s) | Different companies share an office space and common infrastructures such as reception, refreshments and post room. | A turn-up, plug-in and away-you-go convenience. Flexible and shorter terms, ranging from one month to two years. Often design led and inspiring spaces to work from. | Not ideal if you are a business that has lots of visitors or if you want to create your own brand and culture. |

| OPERATING MODEL | WHAT IS IT? | THE BENEFITS | THE CHALLENGES |
|---|---|---|---|
| Serviced office | An office or building that is fully equipped and managed, which then rents individual offices or floors to other companies. | A turn-up, plug-in and away-you-go convenience. Flexible and shorter terms, ranging from one month to two years. Dedicated meeting rooms and other facilities such as washrooms and tea points. | Less flexibility in ensuring the space works for you and reflects the organization's culture. Shared spaces such as meeting rooms need to be booked in advance. The spaces often lack design thinking and are often white walls of nothing. |
| Hub and spoke | A primary HQ (hub) and local satellite offices (spokes) convenient to employee locations. | The best of both worlds. City centre hubs but flexibility for employees to reduce commutes and work closer to home at a spoke. Cost benefits in downsizing city centre primary real estate. The flexibility is a key benefit for fast-growing businesses. | Potential challenges in maintaining company culture and connectedness. Experience gaps between the hub (ivory tower) and the spokes (pop-up tents). Employees will find themselves in teams sitting across various spokes and therefore relying on technology to connect them. |

The golden triangle of HR, IT and Facilities must pull their data together, prevent siloes and provide the organization with a single source of truth. The more data an organization has, the easier the real estate conundrum becomes.

## KEY TAKEAWAYS

- 'Work' is no longer a place we go; it is an activity, a set of tasks, for a given purpose. With strategies and key performance indicators, work is a process for achieving results – it is the output that matters.
- The when and the how we work is up for grabs, but where people work is sometimes outside of anybody's control. The workplace where people thrive is the workplace that is a destination people want to go to; it is physical, virtual or a mix of both.
- The pendulum has swung too far, and the next few years ahead will find it calibrating somewhere in the middle.
- For the majority, there is still a need and a desire for a physical workplace, but that workplace needs to be a destination that people want to go to and the 'why' must be clear.
- Space can accelerate deeper cultural bonds, or it can thwart those ties and break down relationships.
- If you do not measure it, you form an opinion, not a fact, and you do not know what needs to change, why or how.

# REFLECTIONS

- How do people intend to work versus how they actually work?
- What types of spaces are being used and why?
- What are the peaks and troughs in office utilization? When do they occur and why?
- What is the current way of working versus how the future way of working may look?
- Are your people happy? What is the employee churn?
- How is the wellbeing of your people? What is impacting it?
- What is the projected headcount growth of the organization?
- How technologically advanced is the organization?
- How will technology impact the way space is used and the employee experience going forward?
- What are your competitors/the market doing with their people, ways of working, real estate and technology?
- What impact does the way of working have on the climate?
- Are your customers satisfied?
- Are you a fast-paced innovative company or more traditional?
- How strong are your finances?

# CHAPTER 7

# ARGH, THE ROBOTS ARE COMING!

Robots, a pure imitation of life, will always be at a disadvantage when it comes to things that define humanness: love, dreams, creativity, connection.

The premise of the film *I, Robot* is that we must be careful to avoid technology revolution to ensure humans remain in control of the robots. Technology has come a long way, given that one of the first pieces of technology within the workplace was the clocking in/out machine in the late 1800s. Although it helped people get paid, it was mainly used to discipline those showing up late or leaving early. Over time, as technology advanced, it began to affect the humanness of organizations with such time tracking and payroll systems relying on an employee number, instead of a name. Then came CCTV, followed by technology to monitor email and PC use, space utilization sensors and space booking systems.

Although technology has been implemented for the best intentions overall, it has resulted in people in the workplace feeling spied on, monitored and controlled, leaving people suspicious and fearful of workplace technology. In addition, interactions that were once between people have been redirected toward screens, leaving us feeling disconnected. Some would argue that technology has done more to harm the human workplace than to help.

The potential misuse of technology has caused fear for personal, organizational and indeed national security, with artificial intelligence (AI) even having the potential to destroy the world. Stephen Hawking stated that dismissing the implications of highly intelligent machines could be humankind's worst mistake in history:

"One can imagine such technology outsmarting financial markets, out-inventing human researchers, out-manipulating human leaders, and developing weapons we cannot even understand.

> Whereas the short-term impact of AI depends on who controls
> it, the long-term impact depends on whether it can be controlled
> at all."[123]

Bill Gates warned that we should be very careful about AI. "If I had to guess at what our biggest existential threat is, it's probably that. With artificial intelligence, we're summoning the demon."[124] Many of the big names within technology such as Gates and Musk are calling for the use of AI to be regulated to prevent the risk to humanity, with the main concern being that robots could reach a certain level of consciousness and start to redesign themselves and thus advance at faster speeds than the slower-evolving human race. I guess the challenge to the human race is, can we program ethics into a robot?

Now, even writing this is making my head hurt, it feels like a film, so let us come down a few pegs to the fact that technology continues to accelerate on an exponential level, disrupting and driving change globally. There are people running businesses, their lives even, solely from their mobile phones; we can place an order laid in bed and receive it the next day, pay our bills, stay socially connected or control our heating and lighting and check how active we have been during the day. No matter what work we do, our days are filled with reminders of all the ways that technology adoption has driven our experiences on a personal and professional level.

We could panic and worry that our jobs are at risk, but technology can help humans resolve some of our biggest challenges, and we must remember that as of today, technology is as reliant on humans as humans are on technology, so let's hope that the true power of AI is regulated and kept away from any megalomaniacs.

The World Economic Forum (WEF) have declared that robots are actually going to increase human employment, with a net increase of 58 million jobs:

"The fear that machines will render large swaths of people unemployed is vastly overblown. By taking over the drudgery of repetitive tasks and the danger of more perilous ones, automation will free up humans to do more challenging work – interfacing with customers, developing better products, and yes, managing those robots themselves"[125]

The human workplace leverages technology to automate the things that drain, like trying to find a time and place to get a team together, canned responses on emails and other administrative tasks. When technology takes the monotony out of everyday tasks, more time is available for people to connect, collaborate, think creatively, and align roles and interests with company goals. People are able to spend more time engaging with work that inspires and interests them, which in turn increases productivity and overall employee happiness. The right amount of technology can enable people to thrive and our organizations to thrive.

We claim that we are far more connected than ever, and we are in a technological sense, but on a human-to-human level, there is a lack of deep and meaningful connection, one that technology can only dream of replacing (if technology could dream, that is). Technology certainly makes it easier to connect and collaborate, changes the way people work and facilitates remote work, which in turn contributes to and drives new ways of living.

If applied correctly, technology has the ability to positively influence and support humanity through engaging and protecting those we care about and the people who work in organizations.

The human workplace utilizes technology to simplify the flow of people, ideas and emotions, enabling people to be more productive, efficient and innovative, stay connected, and feel safe and cared for.

In the world we now live in, poor or outdated technology limits human experience and exposes people and organizations to cybercrime. There is a large mismatch between the technology we use in our home lives and the hyper-personalization, control and choice, and the technology that is on offer when we are in a physical workplace – lumping around 10kg laptops, paper filing, far too many spreadsheets, relying on humans to do the most basic of tasks, fighting with the office lighting to avoid migraines, and having a similar fight with air conditioning just to avoid shivering or profusely sweating. There is hope though; the number of Internet of Things (IoT) devices worldwide is forecast to triple from 8.74 billion in 2020 to more than 25.4 billion IoT devices in 2030.[126]

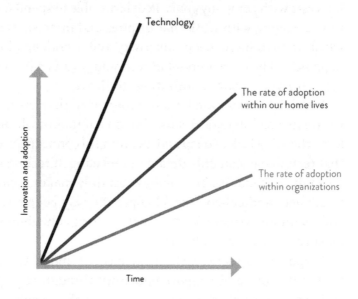

There needs to be an element of replicating and mirroring a person's technology outside of the organization to form a seamless experience between work and life. The most successful businesses will be those that use technology to ensure they remain focused on what matters most – people.

## KEY TAKEAWAYS

- Technology is rising at an exponential rate.
- Technology has the potential to cause more harm than good and needs regulating.
- Society requires increased education in relation to technology available, the future and how to protect yourself / your data.
- Technology should be utilized to enhance the human experience, not replace it.

## REFLECTIONS

- How much technology do you use day-to-day now, compared to ten years ago?
- What aspects of your life could benefit from increased technology?
- What aspects of your work could benefit from improved technology?
- What aspects of your work could be replaced by technology?
- Are you prepared for a future of increased technology?

# CHAPTER 8

# THE HUMAN-CENTRIC WORKPLACE
# PLAYBOOK

The Human-Centric Workplace Playbook offers a set of guiding principles set to inspire and ignite change in the way we work, live and interrelate with each other. It challenges leaders and organizations to create human workplaces for people to thrive, businesses to thrive and leave the planet in a better way than when we arrived,

## THE GUIDING PRINCIPLES

- People are empowered to bring their whole self to work; everybody deserves to be seen, heard and known. We rebel conformity, understand our own uniqueness and bring it to the party and embrace others doing the same.
- Everybody deserves to feel and have those feelings acknowledged. We get to know, really know, the people we work with: what is important to them, what are their idiosyncrasies, hang-ups and dreams – we are all human.
- We embrace and practice curiosity.
- Emotionally intelligent leaders inspire and lead by example.
- Our people deserve the opportunity to develop their skills, use their talents and return home from work each day feeling fulfilled.
- Nobody is merely a means to a company's financial success.
- We practise gratitude, ensuring those around us know they are valued and the reasons why.
- The workspace is wherever people are working from.
- The workplace is where people, technology and space combine.
- The workplace enables communities and connection.
- We listen, continue to learn and evolve.
- The technology is an enabler for our people to achieve.
- Everybody deserves to thrive.
- We are conscious of our impact upon the planet for future generations.

## ACTIVITY: *Rate the humanness of the organization you work for.*

| 1 | 2 | 3 | 4 | 5 | 6 | 7 | 8 | 9 | 10 | Your Score |
|---|---|---|---|---|---|---|---|---|---|---|
| Big ideas are welcomed and will spark creativity from others. | | | | | | | | | Things become stale; any snippet of an idea is quashed as it is "not what we do around here". | |
| People are connected to the purpose and it motivates them to succeed. | | | | | | | | | Staff are more connected to their pay packet and bonuses. | |
| People strive to keep customers happy and ensure they return. | | | | | | | | | Staff see customers as the bane of their lives and are relieved when they say they will not be back. | |
| People put in their best work. | | | | | | | | | Staff turn up, sometimes. | |
| People are comfortable taking measured risks and making mistakes. | | | | | | | | | No risk taking, they are not prepared to be humiliated. | |
| People are trusted to do what they think is best. | | | | | | | | | Staff are questioned over every move. | |
| Morale is high. | | | | | | | | | What's morale? | |
| People are well and thriving. | | | | | | | | | People are ill, stressed and surviving. | |
| People-centric. | | | | | | | | | Organization / finances centric. | |
| It is lovely to work there. | | | | | | | | | You have Sunday evening fear. | |
| Stories are told to engage and inspire. | | | | | | | | | There is toxic gossiping. | |
| It is all about "we". | | | | | | | | | It is all about "me". | |
| Clear expectations and open communication. Regular feedback, positive and negative. Transparency. | | | | | | | | | Bullying and wearing down. Public ridiculing and annual reviews. Insecurity and uncertainty. | |
| Teams, community, and friends. | | | | | | | | | Cliques, departments, and colleagues. | |

| 1 | 2 | 3 | 4 | 5 | 6 | 7 | 8 | 9 | 10 | Your Score |
|---|---|---|---|---|---|---|---|---|---|---|
| Wins are celebrated. | | | | | | | | | Wins are used to ridicule others. | |
| Leaders are visible, accessible, and approachable. | | | | | | | | | You are told to only speak to your direct manager. | |
| The physical workspace is invested in to enable people to thrive. | | | | | | | | | The physical workspace looks like it hasn't been touched since the 60s. | |
| Clear routes of progress to aspire to. Agreed and discussed targets for accountability and responsibility. Continued development of people. Nurturing. | | | | | | | | | You must play golf with the boss. Finger pointing and blame. Annual tick boxes. Stunting of growth. | |
| Equality, Inclusion and Diversity. | | | | | | | | | Everybody looks, talks, sounds, and thinks the same. | |
| Leaders lead by example. | | | | | | | | | Managers can do and say what they like, they are the managers after all. | |
| Hire for culture fit. | | | | | | | | | Hire solely because of their skills. | |
| People speak up. | | | | | | | | | People head to Glassdoor to have a voice. | |
| Reasonable and flexible working schedules. | | | | | | | | | Juggling parenting around an 8am meeting that the boss insisted on, like they do every single day. | |
| You feel valued as a person. | | | | | | | | | You feel like a cog in a machine. | |
| Reward and recognition are in line with efforts. | | | | | | | | | Rewards and recognition are in line with output, and the best way to get what you want is to threaten that you are leaving the organization. | |

## YOUR SCORE

| Score | Category | Appraisal |
|---|---|---|
| 25–50: | Human | Wow – your organization is absolutely rocking it. Give them the certificate and tell them to keep it up! |
| 51–100: | Humanness | Still good, review the problem areas and support your organization to be more human. |
| 101–150: | Cyborg | Hmm, some things are not quite right here. Maybe the rest of this book will help you? |
| 151–200: | Robotic | Well, that is not good. |
| 201–250: | Even the robots would hate it | Oh no. After checking your calculations, take some time to reflect: is this the right place for you? |

# REFLECTIONS:

- How did you score your organization?
- Do you have a colleague you can compare scores with?
- Is the actual culture you are experiencing different from the intended culture?
- What can you do to drive increased humanness in your organization?

# RIGHT,
# LET'S WRAP IT UP

Forming a human-centric workplace where people, communities and our planet thrive is not easy. It takes time, effort and skill, but I promise you, it will be worth it. We all have a part to play, not just senior leadership, but each and every single one of us. We must take responsibility and hold others to account. Are you treating people how you want to be treated?

Each organization is different, with its own makeup, its own challenges, culture, priorities and finances, all of which need to be taken into account. There is no cookie cutter, I am afraid.

I am going to end by saying if we listen, show compassion and empathy, respect our differences and simply uphold the highest levels of integrity, we might just change the world with one small human act at a time.

Thank you for making it to the end and I hope this is just the beginning! – do reach out and share your stories **simone@the-human-centricworkplace.com**

Take care and be a good human.

SFJ

# ENDNOTES

1.  Jung, C. (1946). *Psychological types, or the psychology of individuation.* New York: Harcourt, Brace and Company.

2.  Argyris, C. (1982). *Reasoning, learning and action.* San Francisco, CA: Jossey-Bass.

3.  Hochschild, Arlie. (1979). "Emotion work, feeling rules, and social structure." *American Journal of Sociology*, 551-575.

4.  Natural History Museum. (2021). "Human Evolution." Retrieved from Natural History Museum: https://www.nhm.ac.uk/discover/human-evolution.html

5.  Aristotle. (350 BCE). *Nicomachean Ethics.*

6.  Wittgenstein, Ludwig. (1921). *Tractatus-Logico-Philosophicus.*

7.  Peterson, A. L. (2001). *Being Human: Ethics, Environment, and Our Place in the World.* Oakland, CA: University of California Press.

8.  Gilbert, D. (2007). *Stumbling on Happiness.* New York, NY: Harper Perennial.

9.  Wilcox, C. (2018, October 17). "Human-Caused Extinctions Have Set Mammals Back Millions of Years." Retrieved from National Geographic: https://www.nationalgeographic.com/animals/article/millions-of-years-mammal-evolution-lost-news

10. Attenborough, D. (Director). (2020). *A life on our Planet* [Motion Picture]. Retrieved from David Attenborough, 2020: https://attenboroughfilm.com/

11. Farrar, J. (n.d.). "What Does It Mean to Be Human?" Retrieved from BBC Earth: https://www.bbcearth.com/blog/?article=what-does-it-mean-to-be-human

12. Tutu, Desmond. (2000). *No Future Without Forgiveness.* London: Penguin Random House.

13. Block, P. (2003). *The Answer to How is Yes.* Oakland, CA: Berrett-Koehler.

14. IBM. (2021, February). "A Commitment to Employee Education." Retrieved from IBM: https://www.ibm.com/ibm/history/ibm100/us/en/icons/employeeedu/

15. IBM. (2020). *IBM and Good Tech: Modelling Responsible Stewardship in the Digital Age*. IBM.

16. Carrick, M. (2019). *Bravespace Workplace*. Lambertville, NJ: Maven House.

17. Cox, J. (2017, June). Maiden Speech.

18. Tajfel, H., Turner, J. C., Austin, W. G., & Worchel, S. (1979). "An Integrative Theory of Intergroup Conflict." *Organizational identity: A reader*. 56-65.

19. Rietz, M. and Higgins, J. (2019) *Speak Up: Say what needs to be said and hear what needs to be heard*. Upper Saddle River, NJ: FT Publishing International.

20. Petrou, P., van der Linden, D., Mainemelis, C., & Catalina Salcescu, O. (2020). "Rebel with a Cause: When Does Employee Rebelliousness Relate to Creativity?" *Journal of Occupational and Organizational Psychology*, 811-833.

21. Kaku, D. M. (2014). Behold the Most Complicated Object in the Known Universe. (T. L. Show, Interviewer.) https://www.wnyc.org/story/michio-kaku-explores-human-brain/)

22. Breuning, L.G. (2012). *Meet Your Happy Chemicals*. Scotts Valley, CA: CreateSpace Independent Publishing.

23. Lieberman, D. Z., & Long, M. E. (2018). *The Molecule of More: How a Single Chemical in Your Brain Drives Love, Sex, and Creativity—and Will Determine the Fate of the Human Race*. Dallas, TX: BenBella Books.

24. Lustig, R. H. (2018). *The Hacking of the American Mind*. New York, NY: Penguin Random House.

25. Breuning, L. G. (2015). *Habits of a Happy Brain: Retrain your Brain to Boost Your Serotonin, Dopamine, Oxytocin, & Endorphin Levels*. London: Adams Media.

26. Goleman, D. (2005). *Emotional Intelligence: Why It Can Matter More Than IQ*. New York, NY: Bantam.

27. Siegel, D. (1999). *The Developing Mind*. New York, NY: Guilford Press.

28. Hochschild, Arlie. (1979). "Emotion Work, Feeling Rules, and Social Structure." *American Journal of Sociology*, 551-575.

29. Rogers, Carl R. (1951) Client-centered Therapy: Its Current Practice, Implications and Theory. Boston, MA: Houghton Mifflin

30. McHenry, L. (2018) A Qualitative Exploration of Unconditional Positive Regard and its Opposite Constructs in Coach-Athlete Relationships. Master's Thesis, University of Tennessee. Accessed: https://trace.tennessee.edu/utk_gradthes/5046

31. Shefer, N., Carmeli, A. and Cohen-Meitar, R. (2018), Bringing Carl Rogers Back In: Exploring the Power of Positive Regard at Work. British Journal of Management, 29: 63-81. https://doi.org/10.1111/1467-8551.12247

32. Rock, D. (2008). SCARF: "A Brain-Based Model for Collaborating With and Influencing Others." *NeuroLeadership Journal.*

33. Maslow, A. H. (1943). A theory of human motivation. *Psychological Review, 50*(4), 370–396. https://doi.org/10.1037/h0054346

34. Hertzberg, F., Mauser, B., & Bloch, B. (1959). *The Motivation to Work.* New York, NY: Wiley.

35. McClelland, D. (1961). *The Achieving Society.* Princeton, NJ: Van Nostrand.

36. Vroom, V. (1964). *Work and Motivation.* Oxford: Wiley.

37. McClelland, D. (1961). *The Achieving Society.* Princeton, NJ: Van Nostrand.

38. Herzberg, F. (1964). "The Motivation-Hygiene Concept and Problems of Manpower." *Personnel Administration,* 3-7.

39. Porter, L. W., & Lawler, E. E. (1968). *Managerial attitudes and performance.* Homewood, IL: Irwin Dorsey.

40. Deci, E., & Ryan, R. (1991). "A Motivational Approach to Self: Integration in Personalities." In *Perspectives on Motivation* (pp. 237-288). University of Nebraska Press.

41. Pink, D. (2010). *Drive.* New York, NY: Riverhead Books.

42. Fast, J. (1971). *Body Language.* Lanham, MD: Rowman & Littlefield.

43. Cameron, K. S., Quinn, R. E., DeGraff, J. T., & Thakor, A. V. (2014). *Competing Values Leadership – New Horizons in Management.* Cheltenham: Edward Elgar Publishing.

44. Hofstede, G., Neuijen, B., Ohayv, D. D., & Sanders, G. (1990). "Measuring Organizational Cultures: A Qualitative and Quantitative Study Across Twenty Cases." *Administrative Science Quarterly,* 286-316.

45. Cooke, R., & Rousseau, D. (1988). "Behavioural Norms and Expectations: A Qualitative Approach to the Assessment of Organizational Culture." *Group and Organization Studies,* 245-273.

46. Walker, B., & Soule, S. A. (2017, June 20). "Changing Company Culture Requires a Movement, Not a Mandate." Retrieved from *Harvard Business Review*: https://hbr.org/2017/06/changing-company-culture-requires-a-movement-not-a-mandate

47. Kahn Academy. (2021). "The Origin of Humans and Early Human Societies." Retrieved from: https://www.khanacademy.org/humanities/world-history/world-history-beginnings/origin-humans-early-societies/a/what-were-paleolithic-societies-like#:~:text=Based%20on%20the%20experiences%20of,twenty%20bands%20constituted%20a%20tribe.

48. Bertalanffy, L.V. (1968). *General System Theory.* New York, NY: Braziller.

49. Swann, A. (2018). *The Human Workplace.* London: Kogan Page.

50. Hamel, G. (2014, November 4). "Bureaucracy Must Die." Retrieved from *Harvard Business Review*: https://hbr.org/2014/11/bureaucracy-must-die

51. Bijl, D. W. (2011). *The New Way of Working.* New York, NY: ParCC.

52. Corritore, M., Goldberg, A., & Srivastava, S. B. (2020, January-March). "The New Analytics of Culture." *Harvard Business Review.*

53. Gallup. (2017). *State of the Global Workplace.* Washington, DC: Gallup Press.

54. Wallace, N. (2019). *The Conscious Effect.* London: LID Publishing.

55. Lyubomirsky, S. (2010). *The How of Happiness.* London: Piatkus.

56. Myers, G. D., & Diener, E. (2018). "The Scientific Pursuit of Happiness." *Association for Psychological Science*, 218-225.

57. Jebb, A. T., Tay, L., Diener, E., & Oishi, S. (2018). Happiness, Income Satiation and Turning Points Around the World. *Nature Human Behaviour 2*, 33-38.

58. The World Happiness Report. (2021). "The World Happiness Report 2021." Retrieved from: https://worldhappiness.report/

59. OECD. (2021). "Better Life Index." Retrieved from http://www.oecdbetterlifeindex.org/topics/work-life-balance/

60. Csikszentmihalyi, M. (2002). *Flow.* London: Rider.

61. Denmark, V. (2021, April 3). What Is Hygge? Retrieved from: https://www.visitdenmark.com/denmark/highlights/hygge/what-hygge

62. BITC. (2019). *Mental Health at Work.* London: BITC.

63. Achor, S. (2010). *The Happiness Advantage.* New York, NY: Penguin Random House.

64. Brown, B. (2018). *The Gifts of Imperfection: Let Go Who You Think You're Supposed to Be and Embrace Who You Are.* Center City, MN: Hazelden FIRM.

65. Edmondson, A. C. (2018). *The Fearless Organization: Creating Psychological Safety in the Workplace for Learning, Innovation and Growth.* Hoboken, NJ: Wiley.

66. Google, R. W. (2016). "Guide: Understand Team Effectiveness." Retrieved from re: Work: https://rework.withgoogle.com/guides/understanding-team-effectiveness

67. World Health Organization (2021) "Long working hours increasing deaths from heart disease and stroke" retrieved from: Long working hours increasing deaths from heart disease and stroke: WHO, ILO

68. DeFilippis. E, Impink,S.M, Singell, M,. Polzer,J,T and Sadun, R. (2020) Collaborating During Coronavirus: The Impact of COVID-19 on the Nature of Work. NBER Working Paper No. 27612. Retrieved from: w27612.pdf (nber.org)

69. Siegel, D. (1999). *The Developing Mind*. New York, NY: Guilford Press.

70. Speaker. TedX Talks, A. E. (2014). "Building a Psychologically Safe Workplace." Retrieved from YouTube: https://www.youtube.com/watch?v=LhoLuui9gX8

71. Brown, B. (2012). *Daring Greatly: How the Courage to Be Vulnerable Transforms the Way We Live, Love, Parent, and Lead*. London: Penguin Life.

72. Oxford Economics. (2014). *The Cost of Brain Drain: Understanding the Financial Impact of Staff Turnover*. Chattanooga, TN: Unum.

73. The Institute of Customer Service. (2021). *UK Customer Satisfaction Index*.

74. Ibid.

75. United Nations. (2021). *Global Humanitarian Overview 2021*. United Nations Office for the Coordination of Humanitarian Affairs.

76. OXFAM. (2017). *An Economy for the 99%*. OXFAM.

77. Obama, B. (2016). (U. G. Assembly, Interviewer.)

78. Global Justice Now. (2016). "Corporations vs Governments Revenues." Retrieved from: http://www.globaljustice.org.uk/sites/default/files/files/resources/corporations_vs_governments_final.pdf

79. Crivelli, E., Mooij, R. D., & Keen, M. (2015). "Base Erosion, Profit Shifting and Developing Countries." IMF Working Paper.

80. Tax Justice Network. (2016). "Kenya Losing $1.1bn to Tax Exemptions." Retrieved from: http://www.taxjustice.net/cms/upload/pdf/kenya_report_full.pdf

81. Stockholm International Peace Research Institute. (2021, April 27). "SIPRI for the Media." Retrieved from: Stockholm International Peace Research Institute: https://www.sipri.org/media/press-release/2020/global-military-expenditure-sees-largest-annual-increase-decade-says-sipri-reaching-1917-billion

82. United Nations. (2021). *Global Humanitarian Overview 2021*. United Nations Office for the Coordination of Humanitarian Affairs.

83. *BBC News*. (2020). "Climate Change Cut Carbon Emissions from your Commute." Retrieved from: https://www.bbc.com/future/article/20200317-climate-change-cut-carbon-emissions-from-your-commute

84. *The Carbon Brief*. (2020). "Coronavirus Set to Cause Largest Ever Annual Fall In CO2 Emissions." Retrieved from: https://www.carbonbrief.org/analysis-coronavirus-set-to-cause-largest-ever-annual-fall-in-co2-emissions

85. *Loop*. (2020). "9 Steps that Companies Can Take to Reduce their Carbon Footprint." Retrieved from: https://loopup.com/en/resource-center/blog/responsible-business-travel-9-steps-that-companies-can-take-to-reduce-their-carbon-footprint/

86. *United Nations*. (2020). "Emissions Gap Report 2020: United Nations, 2020." Retrieved from: https://www.unep.org/emissions-gap-report-2020

87. Schwab, K. (2016). *The Fourth Industrial Revolution*. London: Penguin.

88. Barnes, M. (1988). "Construction Project Management." *International Journal of Project Management*, 6 (2) 69-79.

89. Krugman, Paul. (1994). *The Age of Diminishing Expectations*. Cambridge, MA: MIT Press.

90. Thompson, K., & Luthans, F. (2002). *Organizational Culture: a Behavioral Perspective*. McSweeney and Parks.

91. de Berker, A. O., Rutledge, R. B., Mathys, C., Marshall, L., Cross, G. F., Dolan, R. J., & Bestmann, S. (2016). "Computations of Uncertainty Mediate Acute Stress Responses in Humans." *Nature Communications*.

92. Rock, D. (2018, June 7). "Approaching Diversity with the Brain in Mind." Retrieved from Strategy and Business: https://www.strategy-business.com/article/Approaching-Diversity-with-the-Brain-in-Mind

93. Sinek, S. (2017). *Leaders Eat Last: Why Some Teams Pull Together and Others Don't*. London: Penguin.

94. Gallup. (2020). "The Future Top Workplaces Rely on Manager Development." Retrieved from: https://www.gallup.com/workplace/324131/future-top-workplaces-rely-manager-development.aspx

95. Ibid.

96. Peter, Laurence J. (1969). *The Peter Principle*. London: Pan Macmillan.

97. Rock, David. (2009). "Managing with the Brain in Mind." *Psychology Today*. Accessed 13 July 2021. https://www.psychologytoday.com/sites/default/files/attachments/31881/managingwbraininmind.pdf

98. Brown, B. (2015). *Rising Strong: How the Ability to Reset Transforms the Way We Live, Love, Parent, and Lead*. London: Vermilion.

99. Gallup. (2020, June). "Why Leaders Need to Build Trust with Employees." Retrieved from: https://www.gallup.com/workplace/312833/why-leaders-need-build-trust-employees.aspx

100. Freud, S. (1933). *New Introductory Lectures on Psychoanalysis*. London: Hogath Press.

101. Usher, N. (2018). *The Elemental Workplace*. London: LID Publishing.

102. Goleman, D. (1996). *Emotional Intelligence*. New York, NY: Bantam.

103. Davis-Laack, P. (2014). *Addicted to Busy: Your Blueprint for Burnout Prevention*. Stress & Resilience Institute LLC.

104. *People Management*. (2020). "Pandemic Highlights Lack of Soft Skills Among Business Leaders." Retrieved from: https://www.peoplemanagement.co.uk/news/articles/pandemic-highlights-lack-of-soft-skills-among-business-leaders

105. City and Guilds. 2021. "Leading Through Challenging." *ILM*.
Accessed 13 July 2021. https://www.i-l-m.com/-/media/ilm-
website/documents/cg-ilm-leading-through-challenge-report-pdf.
ashx?la=en&hash=A0D9A8B8ACB90EEB5F5D39A2D6325F31CD41A10B

106. Gallup. (2017). *State of the Global Workplace*. Washington, DC: Gallup Press.

107. CIPD. (2020). *Embedding New Ways of Working: implications for the Post
Pandemic Workplace*. London: CIPD.

108. British Council for Offices. (2020). *News: Majority of Workers Plan a Return
to the Office, But Home Working Here to Stay*. 5 October 2020. Accessed 13
July 2021. https://www.bco.org.uk/News/News46982.aspx

109. Institute of Directors. (2020). "News Articles." 5 October 2020. Accessed
13 July 2021. https://www.iod.com/news/news/articles/Home-working-
here-to-stay-new-IoD-figures-suggest

110. UK Data Service. (2020). *Quarterly Labour Force Survey, October-December 2020*.

111. Zuckerberg, M. (2017). Commencement Address at Harvard University.
Retrieved from: https://news.harvard.edu/gazette/story/2017/05/mark-
zuckerbergs-speech-as-written-for-harvards-class-of-2017/

112. Usher, N. (2018). *The Elemental Workplace*. London: LID Publishing.

113. Ibid.

114. Stanford. (2021). "News". 23 February 2021. Accessed 13 July 2021.
https://news.stanford.edu/2021/02/23/four-causes-zoom-fatigue-solutions/

115. Bailenson, J. N. (2021). "Nonverbal Overload: A Theoretical Argument
for the Causes of Zoom Fatigue." Technology, Mind and Behaviour,
Volume 2 Issue 1.

116. Propst, R. (1968). *The Office: A Facility Based on Change*.
Zeeland, MI: Herman Miller Research Corp.

117. Kelley, D., & Kelley, T. (2015). *Creative Confidence: Unleashing the Creative
Potential Within Us All*. London: Harper Collins.

118. Doorley, S., & Witthoft, S. (2012). *Make Space: How to Set the Stage for
Creative Collaboration*. Hoboken, NJ: Wiley.

119. Thaler, H. R., & Sunstein, R. C. (2008). *Nudge: Improving Decision About
Health, Wealth, and Happiness*. New Haven & London: Yale University Press.

120. Usher, N. (2018). *The Elemental Workplace*. London: LID Publishing.

121. Barker, J. (2019). *Paradigms: The Business of Discovering the Future*. New
York, NJ: Harper Business.

122. Panksepp, J. (2004). *Affective Neuroscience: The Foundations of Human and
Animal Emotions*. Oxford: Oxford University Press.

123. Hawking, S., Russell, S., Tegmark, M., & Wilczek, F. (2017, October 23). "Stephen Hawking: 'Transcendence Looks at the Implications of Artificial Intelligence - But Are We Taking AI Seriously Enough?'." Retrieved from Independent: https://www.independent.co.uk/news/science/stephen-hawking-transcendence-looks-implications-artificial-intelligence-are-we-taking-ai-seriously-enough-9313474.html

124. Gates, B. (2015, 29 January). *Washington Post*. Retrieved from: https://www.washingtonpost.com/news/the-switch/wp/2015/01/28/bill-gates-on-dangers-of-artificial-intelligence-dont-understand-why-some-people-are-not-concerned/

125. The World Economic Forum (2021) Retrieved from: https://www.weforum.org/agenda/2021/02/world-economic-forum-automation-create-jobs-employment-robots/

126. Statista, retrieved from: https://www.statista.com/statistics/1183457/iot-connected-devices-worldwide/

# ABOUT THE AUTHOR

With 15 years of experience working within Workplace and Facilities Management, an MBA and a multitude of industry qualifications, Simone Fenton-Jarvis has shaped and nurtured her passion for human-centric workplaces.

Homing in on employee experience, organizational performance, data gathering, change management and business improvement in relation to culture, space, process and technology, Simone wakes up every day on a mission to drive a world where organizations become the vehicle for people and societies to thrive, resulting in us all leaving the planet a better place than when we arrived.

Simone is a well-known face at industry events, so do say hello – she is the introvert in the corner of the room hoping to see a smiley face!

# BOOK SUMMARY

What does it mean to be human? What does it mean to be a human at work? The answer to these questions should not be dissimilar – to have a purpose, to connect and to feel – and yet organizational cultures still do not embrace people bringing their whole selves to work. If we are not showing up, not bringing our whole awesome selves, we are not thriving; we are hiding.

The workplace and leadership are the root cause and fuel of so many societal issues, from wellbeing, the economy, inequality and the climate. Following the year of the largest remote working experiment, not many would argue against work not being somewhere we go but being what we do and the why we do it.

*The Human-Centric Workplace* is about highlighting that we can do better, and we must do better. There are numerous ideas and theories about how and why people are what make organizations thrive (or expire) and yet we still fail to ensure organizations are human-centric.

This all starts with leadership. A person being good at a job does not mean they will be a good leader, and yet organizations continue to promote people, not just past their task performance capability, but past their human management skills capabilities.

Culminating with a playbook, *The Human-Centric Workplace* aims to inform, inspire and drive change through demystifying the 'how' to ensure our people, communities and planet thrive.